The
Superintendent's
Planner

S0-ADV-077

We dedicate this book to Lizzie Brenkus.

Lizzie was the Acquisitions Editor for Corwin Press when we wrote our second book and began this one. Her support, questions, suggestions, and creative ideas inspired this book.

Thank you, Lizzie, for your belief in us.

The Superintendent's Planner

A Monthly Guide and Reflective Journal

Gloria L. Johnston • Rene S. Townsend

Gwen E. Gross • Peggy Lynch • Lorraine M. Garcy

Benita B. Roberts • Patricia B. Novotney

CORWIN PRESS
A SAGE Company

Copyright © 2009 by Corwin Press

All rights reserved. When forms and sample documents are included, their use is authorized only by educators, local school sites, and/or noncommercial or nonprofit entities that have purchased the book. Except for that usage, no part of this book may be reproduced or utilized in any form or by any means, electronic or mechanical, including photocopying, recording, or by any information storage and retrieval system, without permission in writing from the publisher.

For information:

Corwin Press
A SAGE Company
2455 Teller Road
Thousand Oaks, California 91320
www.corwinpress.com

SAGE Ltd.
1 Oliver's Yard
55 City Road
London, EC1Y 1SP
United Kingdom

SAGE India Pvt. Ltd.
B 1/I 1 Mohan Cooperative
    Industrial Area
Mathura Road, New Delhi 110 044
India

SAGE Asia-Pacific Pte. Ltd.
33 Pekin Street #02-01
Far East Square
Singapore 048763

Printed in the United States of America

Library of Congress Cataloging-in-Publication Data

The superintendent's planner : a monthly guide and reflective journal / Gloria L. Johnston . . . [et al.].
    p. cm.
Welcome to the superintendency—July and August: reflecting and getting ready for the new year—September and October: starting smoothly and settling in—November and December: checking in and celebrating progress—January and February: taking stock and planning for next year—March and April: staying focused and facing challenges—May and June: wrapping up and celebrating—The routine and expected—Crises, the unexpected, caveats, and musings—Resource A: school site inspection—Resource B: site readiness inspection sheet—Resource C: summary of school inspections—Resource D: key actions checklist—Resource E: custodian school inspection sheet—Resource F: playground inspections—Resource G: portable building inspections—Resource H: human resource annual calendar—Resource I: meeting schedule—Resource J: administrator evaluation form—Resource K: administrator evaluation process—Resource L: budget guidelines—Resource M: budget calendar—Resource N: planned priorities—Resource O: organization chart—Resource P: information for board members—Resource Q: school district responsibility chart.
  Includes bibliographical references and index.
  ISBN 978-1-4129-6108-0 (cloth)—ISBN 978-1-4129-6109-7 (pbk.)
  1. School superintendents—United States.   2. School management and organization—United States.   I. Johnston, Gloria L., 1947–   II. Title.
  LB2831.72.S875 2009
  371.2'011—dc22   2008021948

This book is printed on acid-free paper.

08   09   10   11   12   10   9   8   7   6   5   4   3   2   1

Acquisitions Editor:	Arnis Burvikovs
Associate Editor:	Desirée A. Bartlett
Editorial Assistant:	Irina Dragut
Production Editor:	Appingo Publishing Services
Cover Designer:	Anthony Paular
Graphic Designer:	Lisa Riley

Contents

Preface

Nearly seven years after finishing my dissertation, titled "A Study of California Superintendents as Instructional Leaders," I attended my state's annual superintendents' symposium, determined that this was the year I would begin to write about the day-to-day work of superintendents. The literature about the work of superintendents that existed was limited and written primarily by university researchers, not practitioners. My goal was to convince some colleagues to write a practical, useful book with me.

At the symposium I shared my short draft book outline with seven practicing and highly respected superintendent colleagues: Rene Townsend, Peggy Lynch, Gwen Gross, Lorraine Garcy, Benita Roberts, Patricia Novotney, and Libia Gil. To my great surprise and delight, they needed no convincing. Each one was enthusiastic and made a commitment to the project.

Over the next three years we met at each other's homes and district offices and in hotel rooms at professional conferences to flesh out the outline and content for this book that would give readers a transparent view into our daily work. We chose to do this by writing stories and sharing the lessons we learned from our experiences.

The biggest challenge was scheduling group meetings since all eight of us were full-time superintendents, managing homes and families, involved in other professional and community affairs, and paying attention to our health. But we did it because we were excited about the project, believed it would help others, and frankly because we were learning so much from each other.

Our organizing structure for the book was through thinking about the people for whom we were responsible: our community, our board, our organization and its people, our students, and ourselves. We laughed and sighed together as we shared our stories with candor, letting the frustration, anxiety, joy, and wisdom of our years of experience emerge in each chapter. We filled a void in the literature about public school superintendents that our colleagues appreciated—those doing the job or aspiring to it, and by those who studied superintendents. A number of our male colleagues commented on our first book, *Eight At The Top: A View Inside Public Education*, published in 2002, telling us they were surprised at how valuable and meaningful the book was to them. Since most education leadership books were written by males, and from a male point of view, they had expected the stories of female superintendents to be very different from theirs. They found that our work is shared regardless of gender or race.

Following the publication of our first book, we knew we had to continue our valuable collaborative experience, so we started a new project. Seven of the original eight laid out the plan for another book, this time focused on what it takes for superintendents and their elected school boards to work together to improve student achievement. Published in 2007, *Effective Superintendent–School Board Practices: Strategies for Developing and Maintaining Good Relationships With Your Board*, was dedicated to school board members across the country. At that time we had collectively worked with 137 board members in sixteen different school districts and were well aware of, and grateful for, the sacrifices and contributions these valuable community members make to the youth of the nation.

In this, our third book, *The Superintendent's Planner: A Monthly Guide and Reflective Journal*, we turned our attention to the increasingly complex and demanding day-to-day work of the superintendent. Surveying current books about superintendents, we decided there was another void. This led to a practical book for aspiring, new, and experienced superintendents; board members; and other school district leaders to help them plan for an entire calendar year, staying focused on the work at hand and simultaneously on the work ahead. Once again we reviewed our and our colleagues' experiences. We analyzed the results of planning well, or the serious consequences when planning and executing fell short. We hope our readers will benefit from the insights we gained from our mistakes and oversights, as well as our successes.

Several of us have retired from the superintendent position but, through our ongoing work in education, know a large number of superintendents are stepping into position for the first time, many with little prior experience or mentoring. We are involved in recruiting, selecting, and coaching new superintendents and providing professional development for them, their board members, and others in their school districts. We plan to use this book as a guide with them and to encourage them to use it as a journal where they can record specific plans and reflections that will influence their course of action throughout the year.

While this book focuses on a yearlong look at the work of the superintendent in managing the day-to-day operations of the district, we truly believe the actions in each chapter are an opportunity for leadership. What you do and how you do it, how you communicate and to whom, and how you spend your time powerfully demonstrates your values and vision—critical elements of leadership.

Our profound hope is that you will enjoy the journey of the superintendent's life and that our book provides you with a practical and usable resource to make the journey perhaps not easier, but more effective and certainly more rewarding. We dedicate this book to you in appreciation for all you do for the students of this country. Like you, we know that public education is the lifeblood of democracy, and your leadership makes the positive difference in millions of students' lives.

Be well and thrive!

—Gloria L. Johnston

Acknowledgments

When deciding whom we should acknowledge in this, our third book written together, we discussed the many professionals who have inspired, guided, and supported us over the years. With nearly ninety years of experience among us and track records of success serving as superintendents in sixteen urban, rural, and suburban school districts, our list was very long.

This book highlights a yearlong look at the work of the superintendent, focusing on day-to-day operations, while stressing that good management forms the foundation for stronger leadership. Nearly every action described in this book involves others in the school district, and they are key to participating in and carrying out decisions, plans, and tasks. Because of the team effort required for successful leadership that results in improved student achievement, we acknowledge and thank the following colleagues:

- Current superintendents we respect and admire
- Retired and deceased superintendents who have mentored and encouraged us
- Our assistant superintendents, directors, coordinators, and district office colleagues who helped shape our work and accomplish much of what we set out to do each year
- Our principals and other site administrators who truly delivered on-the-ground leadership at their schools
- Teacher leaders who have gone above and beyond their responsibilities to improve the quality of teaching and learning in their classrooms and schools

- Our executive assistants, secretaries, and clerks who managed our calendars, read our minds, and supported us in every aspect of our work

These colleagues have been the embodiment of leadership, good communication, and building quality relationships. We are grateful for all they have done for us and for the students in our schools!

Corwin Press gratefully acknowledges the contributions of the following individuals:

Marie Blum
Superintendent
Canaseraga Central School District
Canaseraga, NY

Brenda S. Dietrich
Superintendent
Auburn-Washburn USD 437
Topeka, KS

Robert A. Frick
Superintendent
Lampeter-Strasburg School District
Lampeter, PA

Douglas Gordon Hesbol
Superintendent
Laraway CCSD 70C
Joliet, IL

Dan Lawson
Superintendent
Tullahoma City Schools
Tullahoma, TN

About the Authors

 **Gloria L. Johnston** has devoted over forty years to a career in education. She currently coaches, mentors, and provides professional development for principals, central office administrators, superintendents, and school boards. The focus of her work is on systemic strategies that lead to improving student achievement and closing the achievement gap.

Her years of service in prekindergarten through Grade 12 education included roles as a teacher, principal, central office administrator, and twelve years as a superintendent of schools. She worked in urban, suburban, and rural school districts in Illinois, California, and Caracas, Venezuela. Most recently she served as Dean of the School of Education at National University, headquartered in San Diego, California.

Throughout her career Gloria has been an invited speaker at state and national professional conferences, served on state and national educational and research committees, and has been awarded major professional development grants. She is coauthor of two books, *Eight at the Top: A View Inside Public Education*, a collection of stories about the work of school district superintendents, and *Effective Superintendent–School Board Practices: Strategies for Developing and Maintaining Good Relationships With Your Board*, a practical, experience-based look at the most important role the superintendent has in leading a school district.

Dr. Johnston earned her PhD in Public Policy Analysis from the University of Illinois at Chicago, her MS in Bilingual/Bicultural Education and her BS in Humanities (magna cum laude) from Northern Illinois University. She currently lives in San Diego, California, close to her two children, three grandchildren, and the beach.

Rene S. Townsend is managing partner of Leadership Associates, a superintendent-executive search firm, and executive director of Education Outreach for Price Charities. Previously Rene was a teacher, principal, deputy superintendent, and superintendent for two California school districts.

In addition to coauthoring *Eight at the Top: A View Inside Public Education,* and *Effective Superintendent–School Board Practices* with the current authors, Rene and two colleagues authored *A Practical Guide to Effective School Board Meetings.* She has also written numerous articles and book reviews. Rene chaired the California State Superintendents' Committee and the annual state superintendents' symposium, and has won awards in leadership, curriculum, and peacemaking. She earned her BS from the University of Washington, master's degree from San Diego State University, and doctorate from Northern Arizona University.

Gwen E. Gross served as superintendent at Manhattan Beach Unified School District, Beverly Hills Unified, Ojai Unified, and at the then one-school Hermosa Beach City School District prior to joining the 26,000-student Irvine Unified School District in Orange County, California. In addition to her seventeen years as a superintendent, she has been an elementary and middle grades teacher, principal, director of operations, and faculty member at universities in the Midwest and on the West Coast. She was named as one of the "Top 100 Educators in North America" and was honored as the "2005 Superintendent of the Year" by Pepperdine University, where she has served as an adjunct professor of Education Leadership for ten years.

Dr. Gross is active in many community and professional organizations. She has held leadership positions in many of them, particularly with ACSA, where she has chaired the New Superintendents' Annual Symposium, the 2007 superintendents' symposium, served as the vice chair of the State Superintendents' Committee, and has been named a Tri-County Superintendent of the Year. Together with several other superintendents, Gwen coauthored *Eight at the Top: A View Inside Public Education* and *Effective Superintendent–School Board Practices.* She was a bimonthly columnist for the *Beach Reporter* newspaper serving Los Angeles County's South Bay area, and she has developed a series of creative communication documents for distribution to the many constituencies served by public schools.

Dr. Gross is a graduate of the University of Wisconsin (BA), University of Akron (MA), and Kent State University (PhD), and she received a Post-Doctoral Certificate from Harvard University. Her husband, Jerry, is a retired superintendent, and together they have three adult children.

Peggy Lynch recently retired after serving for nearly seven years as the superintendent of the San Dieguito Union High School District located in the northern part of San Diego County. Prior to San Dieguito she was the superintendent of Brea Olinda Unified School District in Orange County, California. Her career spans thirty-eight years and includes middle and high school teaching, high school assistant principal and principal, and assistant superintendent.

Peggy served on the San Diego County Department of Education Achievement Gap Task Force, as well as other county advisory committees. She was also cochair of the San Diego and Imperial counties superintendents group for ACSA (Association of California School Administrators). She has chaired the Superintendents' Symposium Committee for ACSA, as well as chaired the organization's annual conference. In Orange County she also chaired the County Superintendents' organization. Her memberships include Southern California Superintendents, Suburban School Superintendents, American Association of School Administrators, and Association of California School Administrators.

She received her undergraduate degree from Parsons College in Iowa; her master's from California State University, Fullerton; and her doctorate from the University of La Verne. Peggy and her husband, Ed, have been active in the arts and live in beautiful San Clemente, California.

Lorraine M. Garcy is the president of LMG Consulting, which provides coaching, mentoring, and professional development for superintendents, school boards, and school administrators. For the past few years Lorraine has been consulting with ACSA, UC Santa Cruz New Teacher Center, and Springboard Schools. She coordinated a grant from the Bill and Melinda Gates Foundation to provide professional development for superintendents, is a member of the design team for Executive Leadership Coaching for superintendents, and is a consultant/coach of the regional Executive Leadership Centers.

Her career in education spans thirty-four years, including fourteen years as a California superintendent in three districts. She received her bachelor's degree from the University of New York, Oswego; a master's degree from the University of California, Santa Barbara; and a doctorate from the University of Southern California. She currently lives with her husband, Tom, in Discovery Bay, California.

Lorraine has coauthored two books, *Eight at the Top: A View Inside Public Education*, in 2002, and *Effective Superintendent–School Board Practices*, published in September 2006.

In 2003 the California State Assembly recognized Dr. Garcy for her service to the students of the State of California with an Assembly Resolution.

Benita B. Roberts retired as superintendent of a 20,000-student California school district in July 2001, where she served for eight of her thirty-four years in public education. Prior to her tenure as a superintendent she was a classroom teacher and held several administrative positions, including assistant superintendent, education services. Since retirement she has spent time in interim administrative assignments, teaching classes in the administrative services credential program at California State University, San Bernardino, and serving as the human resources manager in her family's business.

Ms. Roberts is a second generation Californian and has lived her entire life in the Inland region. She received her undergraduate education at the University of California, Riverside, and a graduate degree from California State University, San Bernardino. She also completed coursework in the University of La Verne's doctoral program in Organizational Management. As superintendent, an especially memorable occasion was her appearance in Washington, D.C., on a televised town hall meeting with the then U.S. Secretary of Education, Richard Riley, on the subject of early college preparation programs.

During her years as a school administrator she served on several community boards, including the Rotary Club of Jurupa, where she completed a year as president. In addition she was a member of the boards of the Jurupa Chamber of Commerce, the Riverside YMCA, United Way of the Inland Valleys, the American Heart Association, and the Jurupa Mountains Cultural Center. Currently she is a member of the board of the Community Foundation serving Riverside and

San Bernardino counties, the Riverside Community College Gateway to College Charter School, and the Riverside Community College Foundation as chair of the finance committee.

The University of California, Riverside, recognized her as an Alumna of Distinction for her community service. Other awards include the Jurupa Chamber of Commerce Citizen of the Year, a Jurupa Council PTA Honorary Service Award, Riverside YWCA Woman of Achievement, and the Jurupa Chamber of Commerce Member of the Year. The Riverside African American Historical Society honored her extended family for their numerous accomplishments as pioneers in the Inland region. In addition to her community work, Benita enjoys gardening. Her home was one of six featured on a recent Riverside Flower and Garden Show tour.

 **Patricia B. Novotney** is an associate professor at the University of La Verne in the department of Organizational Leadership. In addition, she serves as chair of the Professional Administrative Services Credential Program. She is also a consultant with school districts in the areas of governance team training, leadership development, strategic planning, and organizational development. Previously she spent thirty-six years in public school district service. The majority of her work was in school administration as a principal in three Southern California school districts and superintendent in two California school districts, where she served for thirteen years.

Dr. Novotney has also been an adjunct professor teaching masters and doctoral-level classes at Pepperdine University, the University of Southern California, Chapman University, and the California State University campuses at Fullerton, Long Beach, and San Bernardino.

During her time as district superintendent, Dr. Novotney served as president of the Rotary Club and held offices in several other service clubs. She was also active in the Temecula, California, Chamber of Commerce. One of her community passions was her role as president of a nonprofit organization designed to work on the elimination of child abuse. She has received awards from the Rotary, Kiwanis, and Soroptimist clubs; the Temecula Chamber of Commerce and Police Department; and the California State Parent Teacher Association.

Dr. Novotney received her BS degree from Bloomsburg State University, Pennsylvania, where she was awarded the Distinguished

Alumni Service Award in 1994. She received her MS degree in Educational Administration from Chapman University, Orange, California, and her doctoral degree in Institutional Management from Pepperdine University, Los Angeles, California.

She resides in La Quinta, California, with her husband, Jerrold.

1

Welcome to the Superintendency

Among the most accomplished and fabled tribes of Africa, no tribe was considered to have warriors more fearsome or more intelligent than the mighty Masai. It is perhaps surprising then to learn the traditional greeting that passed between Masai warriors, "Kasserian ingera" . . . means "and how are the children?"

—Excerpt from a speech by Rev. Dr. Patrick O'Neill

Introduction

For all of us, it is about the children. What can we do as educational leaders to ensure that the children are always at the forefront? Superintendents really care about their students; they want the best teaching and learning experiences for each one. However, times have changed and the superintendent's scope of work is broader than ever. We may not always take the time to stop and ask how the children are.

That is why when we began the discussions about writing our third book, we talked about the number of new superintendents coming into the position. We were, and remain, concerned about how to prepare people for the role and its many challenges. Perhaps because we are all baby boomers and because we recognize the sheer number of retirements and new hires of superintendents over the next few years, we wanted to write a practical book that could help all new superintendents. However, we also realized that even experienced superintendents need and want support for managing the day-to-day work of this very complex position. What we also know is that managing well helps you lead more effectively.

As a group we all believe school superintendents play powerful roles in shaping the environment for student learning. While many people in education have long understood this to be true, research to support the premise has not always been evident. Our beginning discussions included the recent research by Mid-continent Research for Education and Learning (McREL), which directly tied student achievement to district leadership. Their analysis noted that "effective superintendents focus their efforts on creating goal-oriented districts."

McREL identified five district-level responsibilities that had a significant correlation with student achievement. The five areas are collaborative goal setting, non-negotiable goals for achievement and instruction, board alignment and support of district goals, monitoring goals for achievement and instruction, and use of resources to support achievement and instruction goals.

Significant for superintendents, the research also found that superintendent tenure is positively correlated with student achievement. This is good news for people in this challenging role and should be an important message for school boards around the country. Whether boards of education have three, five, seven, or more members, superintendents know how the board's relationship with them can expand or shorten their contract time with a school district. So how does the superintendent ensure his or her tenure lasts for many years? The answer is doing many things well in a complex position full of amazing subtleties, and doing them with insight, patience, resilience, tact, and a great sense of humor.

As we thought about what had helped us achieve success in our districts, we reflected on what good leadership is. Each of us has been a student of leadership, interested in what we do well ourselves, but also in helping others develop their own leadership styles and vision. We wanted this book to center on five areas we believed essential to a great superintendency focused on student achievement: building relationships, planning/implementing, communicating, monitoring/revising, and coaching/mentoring.

Building Relationships

Intuitively we all know that successful leaders spend much of their time building great relationships with the people in their organizations. They consciously work at understanding the needs and strengths of colleagues with whom they work.

In *The Leadership Secrets of Santa Claus*, the authors note, "You can't possibly focus on your mission without also focusing on the folks that make your mission happen. . . . And besides, since you manage *things* and lead *people*, common sense suggests that it's *people* who are at the core of all leadership activities" (Harvey et al., 2003, p. 14). If we believe this to be true, the work you will do as superintendent must focus on developing, interacting with, and creating a quality work environment for your staff, your board and, most importantly, for your students.

Planning/Implementing

The wise adage—"Fail to plan, plan to fail"—reminds us of the importance of organizational goals, strategies to achieve those goals, and action steps to get things done. In education we are constantly planning for the next event, meeting, achievement target, etc. Good superintendents do this almost without thinking. Great superintendents not only have a plan with goals and targets, they know how they will implement the plan. They also understand how good planning helps them deal with the unexpected events that inevitably occur.

Each of us has been in situations where we had not planned as thoroughly as we should have. These experiences were not pleasant, and we often ended on a frustrated note. We have observed others in our organizations who may not have prepared for a speech or presentation, leaving them and us embarrassed. The action steps and calendar ideas in this book are designed to help you avoid those mistakes.

Communicating

We are only successful in these roles when we communicate effectively to all of our constituencies in ways that will meet the needs of our audiences. While all superintendent communications should reflect your vision for the district, when you are speaking to parents, using too much educational jargon leaves them feeling confused and disconnected. Staff members do not want to be, and should not be, talked down to at any time. Knowing when and how to deliver a certain kind of message is an essential element of good communication.

We each recalled a piece of written communication that went out with a misspelling or a misused word at least once in our careers. Each of us also remembered the one or two (maybe more, depending on the misspelled word) messages back from a parent or board member about the misuse. Planning for, reviewing, and critiquing what you write or say is critical to how you are perceived and whether you are able to effectively communicate the district vision and garner the support you need to achieve that vision.

Monitoring/Revising

Good planning, effective communication, and great relationships can be derailed if you allow plans to move along without checking on their progress. Through monitoring and review, you frequently recognize the need to revise the plans or implementation process. Do not be afraid to admit the need for change.

Throughout any implementation process, factors and contexts may shift. What seemed like a good idea in the quiet of summer planning may not be appropriate in December and January. Involving your district partners (parents, community, staff, students, and the board) early and frequently in the process pays off in assessing what has gone well and what needs redirection.

Coaching/Mentoring

You are the lead teacher in the school district, a role you must take seriously. You model what you expect of others, and you develop the talents of everyone in your organization. Ask yourself: What is the district succession plan? Who are we developing to be our future principals, our next assistant superintendents, and the next superintendent in this or another district?

People watch nearly every move the superintendent makes. How you spend your time is examined. You are the model for people inside the district and often in the community. Spend time coaching those with whom you work; develop a specific plan together to improve their skills. Help your staff try new methods, think through how to handle problems differently, and examine their practices and behaviors. This will enrich the organization while assisting individuals with professional and personal growth.

About the Book

We hope we have gained wisdom and put it in a simple, straightforward format. We wrote this book to help you manage and lead the districts you serve. While the idea of a month-to-month planning book for teachers and principals is not new, such a planning model for superintendents is. Frequently those writing books about the superintendent's work are professors or doctoral students who lack our practical experience. These books focus on theoretical ideas about leadership in systems and thoughts about what the job ought to be. This book is practical; it is about how to organize our work to achieve district goals.

With over ninety years of experience as superintendents in urban, suburban, and rural districts of 1,000 to 50,000 students across California, we are proven, realistic planners and successful implementers. We have written two other books, *Eight at the Top: A View Inside Public Education* and *Effective Superintendent–School Board Practices: Strategies for Developing and Maintaining Good Relationships with Your Board*. One of us, with two colleagues, wrote *A Practical Guide to Effective School Board Meetings*. All of these books were based on knowing theory translated into practice. We have led districts through far-right religious challenges and huge student growth, as well as declining enrollment, and managed to work effectively with over 120 school board members.

The number of new superintendents is growing across the United States, and there are many superintendents who change jobs every year. One of our reviewers noted that in New York almost a third of the superintendents had been on the job for eighteen months or less. While variations exist across the country, the work of the superintendent consists of many common issues—budget, communications, board relationships, development of staff, parent and community relationships, and, most important, student achievement.

This practical book is designed to help you plan for and anticipate the patterns of the superintendent's work. A yearlong calendar serves several purposes for you as a superintendent. First, it demonstrates understanding of the whole operation of the district. Second, it shows how various components connect to each other. Finally, the predictable events can be overlaid with the timelines for preplanning that must occur leading up to the various events.

Through a format of two-month spans, the book provides a series of examples, monthly themes, tasks and tips for the sixty days, and some ideas for thinking ahead. The idea is to keep you focusing on the day-to-day work at the same time you are thinking ahead, keeping the immediate work connected to achieving long-term goals. Throughout each chapter you will have space for reflection on what you have read, how it may differ for you, and what you need to think about for the future.

Whether you are a new superintendent, an experienced superintendent going to a new district, or a veteran with five or more years, you need a sense of the flow for the year ahead. A superintendent new to this complicated and challenging role might want to use the book's contents as a checklist to examine what can be anticipated throughout the year to help plan for the ebbs and flows.

If you are starting your second or third superintendency in a new district, you can use the book as a resource to remind you of how things can be done differently from district to district. Your reflections throughout the chapters will help you in each subsequent year. With that in mind, this book is intended to be a practical resource guide with specific, concrete tasks and tips for completing them in a month-to-month format, at whatever the stage of your career as a superintendent.

Using a yearlong calendar approach, you, as superintendent, help your entire organization. You provide the board with an understanding of the complexity of your work and insights into the integration of so many responsibilities. The approach also enables your administration to see the big picture of the entire district. When administrators and board members know what they might anticipate, the unexpected can be more manageable.

July and August open the book because school districts around the country typically operate on a July–June fiscal pattern, and often new superintendents start their jobs in July. In Chapter 2, Reflecting and Getting Ready for the New Year, you will learn about the importance of taking care of yourself and your family and also taking time to think about how to get organized, be prepared, and develop the strategies to focus your work for the upcoming year.

Chapter 3 deals with September and October and addresses how to start smoothly and settle in to the year. We highlight the importance of communication, politics, and visibility as you set the tone for the year. For November and December, Chapter 4, Checking In and Celebrating Progress, the emphasis is on building the board team and monitoring the budget, programs, and student achievement goals. Taking Stock and Planning for Next Year is the title of Chapter 5, and covers January and February. Here we begin the budget development process for the coming fiscal year, review curriculum, establish new goals, and communicate regarding any new focus areas and priorities.

March and April can seem like long months full of potential distractions, so it would be appropriate to suggest ideas for staying focused and facing new challenges in Chapter 6. We look at long-range planning, budgeting, and personnel actions as well. In Chapter 7 we move to May and June, centered on assessing results and wrapping up. These months are filled with budget work, celebrations, evaluations of staff and the year, and both ending the year and ramping up for the new one.

Over the course of the year's work, we recognize that there are tasks that never end. Chapter 8 addresses those activities that are recurring and typical of the routines that fill the superintendent's days. We look, for example, at the role meetings play virtually every day. While some of this chapter will repeat various key actions discussed in previous chapters, it is done to stress the importance of handling these routine tasks efficiently and effectively.

From the routine, we move to Chapter 9 to consider those unexpected and unusual events that are an inevitable part of being a superintendent. Each of us has handled disasters—natural and human-made. We know that how we handle the really tough situations can make or break the perceptions of those in the organization and in the community about our skill and effectiveness. The Resources section starting on page 81, includes various resources we felt could help any superintendent—new or experienced.

Caveats

We acknowledge that depending on where you are in the country, the months you do some of the outlined action steps will vary since calendars across the United States are different. Your budget process may depend on the action of the state legislature or require a community process. When you are evaluated or when you evaluate your staff may be determined by contract or law. Dates for dismissal of staff may occur earlier or later than the March time period we indicate. School board elections may not occur in November as described in this book. Whatever the variations might be, this book should help any superintendent examine the tasks that need to be done in any school district and in any school year. We also know that you personally may not take every action step, but you will be expected to make sure things get done.

You never develop the calendar and rarely do the activities in isolation. In a small district, you may only have a secretary to help. In a large district, you may have an entire cabinet of administrators. Developing the calendar of activities is strengthened with the broadest input.

You have an opportunity to write your personal action steps at the end of each chapter. You are encouraged to make notes to move these actions to other months or to note who will be responsible for them, but they are still necessary steps in whatever months they fall and by whomever you designate to achieve them.

From Us

While the book focuses on a yearlong look at your work in managing the day-to-day operations of the district, we truly believe that each of your actions is an opportunity for leadership. What you do, how you communicate, and where you spend your time will powerfully demonstrate your values and vision—major elements of leadership.

We wish you joy in your journey as superintendent and hope that our book will provide you with a practical and usable resource to make the journey easier. We appreciate all you do for the students of this country because we know that public education is the lifeblood of democracy. Be well and thrive!

2

July and August

Reflecting and Getting Ready for the New Year

During my first year as a superintendent, I rarely exercised, began to gain weight, and hated the way I felt physically. I had to do something.

—Johnston et al., 2002

July and August are typically thought of as vacation months for educators. In fact, they are a busy and important time to take stock of the prior year and make sure everything is in place to begin a new school year—with all employees focused on improving student achievement and support systems and resources aligned and ready to go on the first day. The looking back and the planning forward that you do during this time will serve you well throughout the year ahead. You will have learned from prior successes and disappointments and used this learning to lead the staff in realizing the district's vision, mission, and goals.

Renewing and refreshing yourself during this time is critical. Make sure you are healthy, organized, and prepared to be an effective leader for your district and the community.

Organizing and Preparing for the Year

Close the door to your office. This is the time of year to spend some quality time at your desk by yourself, thinking, planning, and organizing. Then spend time with your administrative assistant. Make sure any files you keep in your office, as well as those of your administrative assistant, are purged and organized. Meet with your administrative assistant and talk about how and when you will communicate during the year and who will keep which documents.

Make sure the two of you are in tune with how you will manage phone calls, appointments, walk-ins, emails, and hard copy mail. As the front-line person, your administrative assistant is critical in creating effective communication within the school district and with members of the community. You may want her or him to "keep" your calendar and sort and prioritize your mail each day so you will have more time for face-to-face communication. Having a plan for handling phone calls and drop-in visitors gives your assistant authority to act and gives you time for other work.

This is also a good time to review your calendar from the previous year to consider the timing of major activities and actions and determine possible revisions for the coming year. Keeping a file of events, activities, actions, and major topics of the year is a valuable resource when it is time for reflection and planning. You may want to bring those who report directly to you together for this activity to make sure everyone has input into the calendar and that it reflects systemwide timing of major work and events. You and those you work closely with will need to agree upon target dates for projects and assessment of progress.

Spend some time reviewing each of your departments' plans for the new year in order to consider how you will be involved in supporting the administrators and their goals. If you are new to the district, this is a critical time to meet with district administrators to learn about their roles, responsibilities, areas of focus, results from the prior year, and the goals they have set for the coming year.

Determine what needs to be done to ensure that all new employees will be well prepared for their roles as they join this dynamic district. Reaffirm who is responsible for seeing that ongoing work such as curriculum development, professional development, or maintenance and construction plans are established and stay on target. Put dates on your calendar to serve as benchmarks in each of these areas as reminders for you throughout the year. Although specific accountability and monitoring activities are delegated, their accomplishment is your responsibility.

Key Actions

- Clean out your files and desk; ask your administrative assistant/secretary to do the same
- Review last year's calendar and consider revisions and additions
- Prepare your personal calendar/PDA for the year
- Review your personal organization system
- Meet with district-level administrators and review department accomplishments and preview action plans for the new year
- Determine dates for all internal district meetings for the year
- Determine your agenda and discussion topics for your first meetings of the year with principals, teachers, classified staff, board members, parents, and community members
- Publish annual mandatory legal notices
- Review and update student and personnel board policies

Taking Care of Yourself and Your Family

This is usually the best time of the year to take a deep breath, reflect on the year behind you, and review your plans for the year ahead. Most of your students and staff (some may be in summer school), and probably even your board members will take some time for vacation. Phone calls and emails usually slow down, as do community meetings and events. Even if you are a new superintendent, it is a good time for you to get away from the office for some rest and relaxation before the new school year begins.

Now is the time for you to focus on your physical condition and plan for the year ahead. Maintaining your personal health is a rarely discussed element of leadership. Your fitness plan needs to be an integral part of your overall plan for the year ahead. Take time to discuss with your family other personal vacations you would like to take during the coming year and develop a schedule for family events and activities. Once the school year begins, you will find it easier to cancel a date you are holding than to add one to a full calendar. This will allow you to keep you and your family as an important priority in the midst of demands from multiple constituencies.

Key Actions

- Plan to leave town for at least part of your vacation time
- While on leave, turn off your cell phone and computer

- Designate a person to serve as "acting superintendent" while you are gone
- Tell only your administrative assistant, your designee, and the board president where you can be reached
- Develop an exercise plan for the year—and start it now
- Calendar family vacations or special events for the year
- Schedule your annual physical

Ensuring Schools Are Ready to Open

A successful school opening sets a positive tone for the year. Plan carefully for the smooth opening of each school campus. As you think about the opening of the new year, consider all of the elements that go into making a successful opening of school. Be sure you have a plan in place to inspect the schools for readiness. Use a comprehensive checklist for campus walkthroughs that includes the physical plant as well as personnel, orientations, instructional supplies, and materials, and have a clear process determined for following up on anything that may interfere with an effective opening.

Be sure you and your district-level administrators will be on specific campuses, covering all of them, at least the first day or two. School site administrators welcome your support to troubleshoot and ensure student and staff needs are met for students as they start a new school year.

Before the first day of school it is a good idea to review the protocols for visiting school campuses with board members and all school administrators. It is not uncommon, especially at the beginning of the school year, for parents, board members, or other community members to make special requests of principals or teachers that might be unintentionally disruptive or inappropriate. Clarification of protocols contributes to a smooth opening day.

Communicate with local city officials, as well as police and fire departments, about the opening of school and have established clear lines of communication with them for that day and the future. Consider making an appointment with them in their offices to discuss any issues or concerns they have, ask to attend one of their regularly scheduled staff meetings, or take them to lunch to build relationships. They are key players in working with you to address any day-to-day events as well as crises that occur in your schools or the community. You will want to make sure you know how to reach one another quickly and communicate effectively.

Also, take time to review cooperative agreements the district has with other public agencies in the community such as park and recreation districts or social services. Ask for their suggestions for improvements and new ideas. Often modifications are needed based on facility use or available space.

No matter what the size of your district, you must be ready to welcome new employees to your organization. A critical ingredient of that welcome is a thorough orientation that assists new members in becoming a part of the district as quickly as possible, which includes their learning about the history, culture, and organization of the district, and most important, their roles and responsibilities and how they will contribute to meeting the district's student achievement goals.

Updating your district's emergency contact information, processes, and chain of command is vitally important. Be sure you are current regarding the state and federal emergency response mandates. All critical information must be in order and readily accessible: employee phone contact information; the contact information for major service providers such as police, fire, hospitals, gas, water, electrical; community communication sources including radio, newspaper, television; and, of course, local elected officials.

The emergency contact process must include how and what to communicate to parents regarding emergencies and potential school closures. This is a good time to coordinate with your community service and emergency response providers and set a date for a mock disaster drill early in the school year.

Key Actions

- Determine a process to inspect schools for readiness and prepare documentation and procedures for follow up as needed
- Update and revise emergency contact information and procedures
- Review/revise disaster preparedness plans and emergency services
- Calendar a date to conduct a mock disaster exercise during the school year
- Review safety plans for each school campus
- Finalize plans for school registration, transportation, and food service plans
- Finalize new student orientation plans

- Ensure a detailed, inspiring new staff orientation is ready for presentation prior to the beginning of the school year that includes information regarding the history, culture, and organization of the district
- Ensure new staff are well informed about the roles and responsibilities of their positions and how they are expected to contribute to the goals of the district
- Identify and assign mentors/coaches for new staff as needed
- Determine what district-level staff will do to support opening day and clarify responsibilities and assignments
- Review with the school board members and school administrators protocols regarding campus visits from parents, board, and community members
- Communicate with city officials, police, fire, etc., regarding opening day and provide them with a calendar of events for the school year
- Review cooperative agreements with other agencies for any necessary or desired modifications
- Finalize the list of staff to be evaluated during the year and the process to be used

Reviewing Board Policies

Shaping up board policies is an onerous, even Herculean task. Yet it is a job a superintendent can use to move a district toward a higher level of professionalism. The fact was, in my new district, the policies I could find were last updated twenty years earlier. The majority of existing policies had little or no value, and were often contradictory with current law.

—Johnston et al., 2002, p. 49

Without vigilance, board policies quickly become out of date. Take some time to determine policies that need to be reviewed, updated, or added, and develop a calendar with timelines that reflects an efficient process to accomplish this task. Be sure to review your supporting administrative regulations at the same time.

In particular, this is a good time to review your board policy and administrative regulations for holiday celebrations in the district. Revisions made at this time could save you from facing upset students, staff, parents, and community members during those holiday times. You might also want to review your board meeting calendar for the year at this time and look for any potential future conflicts with school or community events. Take any recommended meeting date changes to the board as soon as possible.

Key Actions

- Review board policies and administrative regulations that need to be updated and develop a calendar with timelines for revisions and additions and for presentation for approval at board meetings
- Pay special attention to the board policy and administrative regulations for holidays and special events

Focusing on the Year Ahead

Each year I have developed a district "Word for the Year." This word has been communicated at the beginning of the year kick-off meetings and has been put on districtwide internal memos and all publications. It serves as a reminder of what our focus is. Teachers use this theme in classrooms, and district departments have visual reminders throughout their work environment. Some of these words through the years have been words like Team, Glue, Together, Gold, Personal Best, Commitment, Hustle, Plus, Focus, Results, and Expectations.

—Johnston et al., 2002, p. 68

Finally, as you spend quality time thinking about the new year, consider the major themes that emerge from the district-adopted goals. It is very easy to lose track of the most important goals when the school year begins and hundreds of ideas and requests come your way. Sharing the major themes through your speeches, writings, and conversations helps everyone in the district stay focused on the most important work ahead and makes it more likely the goals will be accomplished.

Meet with individual board members to discuss the themes; make sure they understand them clearly and how they are connected to the board-adopted goals. Most important, make sure the board members are prepared to share the themes with the community at large. A simple one-page handout is helpful for board members when they attend community meetings and events.

Review the best way to communicate with board members individually throughout the coming year. Some board members are content with email communication or a weekly written update from the superintendent. Some prefer face-to-face meetings in the office, and others find a monthly breakfast or lunch date works best for them. Assure them you are committed to sharing all information with all board members and are dedicated to accomplishing the goals they have adopted for the district.

Mentoring and coaching members of the leadership team is an ongoing process for all superintendents. The beginning of a new year is a good time for you to revisit the strengths and growth areas of your team members and consider how you will work with each person in a way that helps them be the best leaders possible. Throughout the year, you can find ways to address their learning needs in a variety of settings, and you will be serving as a role model for them in their daily work with other district staff members.

For administrators who need significant support, consider hiring an external coach who can dedicate focused mentoring and support. Be vigilant in dealing fairly, professionally, and legally in case problems persist and you need to make a leadership change.

Key Actions

- Write speeches and letters that convey your broad themes and goals; communicate these throughout the year
- Finalize details of "Welcome Back" retreats or workshops for all staff and various subgroups
- Assess professional development needs of the leadership team
- Determine dates for leadership team retreats or workshops for the entire year and begin to plan content based on the needs of the team
- Plan activities for meetings and include team-building activities; include others in planning and carrying out professional development
- Develop your plan to mentor and coach new administrators

Speaking From Experience

Most people inside and outside the school district assume that not much happens during the months of July and August. As you can see by the list of action steps for this chapter, when it comes to the work of the superintendent, that is a false assumption. What you accomplish and set in place these two months sets the tone for the entire school year. While the phones and emails may slow down briefly during this period, the relationship building, planning and implementing, communicating, and mentoring and coaching intensify as the new school year begins. Wise superintendents take this time to plan, plan, plan and reap the benefits throughout the remainder of the year.

Upon Reflection

My leadership actions for July and August will be . . .

Building relationships _____

_____

_____

Planning/implementing _____

_____

_____

Communicating _____

_____

_____

Monitoring/revising _____

_____

_____

Coaching/mentoring _____

_____

_____

3

September and October

Starting Smoothly and Settling In

When I accepted a position as a superintendent, I knew how important "showing up" would be to my success and to the success of the organization.

—Johnston et al., 2002

September and October establish the tone for the school year. The major focus of these two months is student learning supported by great teaching. This is a wonderful time of new beginnings, providing you many opportunities for symbolic leadership. Seize the time to kick the year off on the right foot by communicating, being visible, and demonstrating your support for staff.

The real work of the superintendent during these two months is to communicate the messages that are critical for the year. You work to ensure that teachers, classified staff, and site administrators understand the number one goal for everyone is teaching and learning. No matter what their job, they are vital to the success of students.

As superintendent you are responsible for ensuring that the evaluation processes to be used for all staff are understood and set into motion. Your own work with those who report directly to you will model what you expect of your leadership staff. By highlighting the evaluation process you are making it clear to others that ongoing improvement and assessment are essential to making our schools better.

Opening Year Communication

Information should flow steadily during the fall months. Student data are widely shared with principals, teachers, the board of education, and the community. Administrators are learning about staff evaluation expectations from you and/or personnel departments. It is also important for you to communicate with the board about the opening of school, keeping them informed about successes and challenges.

Typically this is the time for initial meetings with parent groups, union leaders, community organizations, and administrative leaders in the district.

Media relations are also important in September and October. Have in mind responses to the typical questions you will be asked at this time of the year. Be prepared to answer questions from the press about how school opened, the challenges, the successes, and your aspirations for the year.

Using this time to communicate your key messages is a regular part of all you do and will establish the tenor for the year. Use every opportunity with the board, parents, staff, and the community to talk about accomplishments, goals, and hopes for the new school year, communicating the vision you and the board have for your students.

Key Actions

- Review and share student achievement results from the previous year with principals, staff members, the board, parents, and the community
- Post student achievement data on your district Web site
- Report on school opening to the board and the community in writing, on your Web site, and in newsletters
- Share feedback and appreciation with those who did the hard work preparing schools for a successful opening
- Develop key points about achievement, budget, and facilities that you want to share with every constituency

- Convene your first meetings with staff, parents, community members, union leaders, and administrators
- Hold your first principals' meeting to share issues, concerns, and accomplishments from the school opening
- Reach out to the media to share the excitement of school starting and to set the tone for the year

Evaluating Staff

The importance of evaluation can never be underestimated. How many times have you heard about an ineffective staff member, but, when you review their evaluations, they are glowing, or worse, nonexistent? This should not happen. Without question, poor or nonexistent evaluation procedures make your life as the superintendent more difficult and do not serve the students well.

During September and October you have the opportunity to share your goals for the year, helping staff understand your expectations, as well as those of the board. You also play an essential leadership role in the evaluation process, because you are modeling how to evaluate and are coaching your staff on effective strategies for improvement.

Key Actions

- Communicate clear expectations and processes for staff evaluation
- Ensure all district and site administrators understand the evaluation procedures for teaching and support staff
- Ensure all staff have been notified regarding evaluation timelines
- Discuss with all administrators the process for their evaluations
- Review any employees about whom other administrators have concerns
- Meet with new administrators to review goals and expectations for their assignment
- Ask board members for feedback on those you directly supervise and evaluate
- Review prior evaluations of those who report directly to you
- Meet with each person whom you evaluate to discuss the year's goals

School Board Elections

When there is a pending school board election, politics can play a large part of these two months. Superintendents are never fond of election season. Elections distract your attention from many areas of importance to you. However, not paying attention to what goes on can be detrimental. You have significant responsibilities with staff and the board throughout the campaign, the election, and the aftermath, and you walk a fine line between involvement and staying out of the political arena.

You have to behave appropriately and legally, of course, and you must help administrative staff do the same. An excellent practice is to provide clear, concise materials regarding the school district in an equitable manner for all board candidates. Sharing this kind of information with the candidates and with staff can present a clear message about the district, not only to those running, but also to the entire community.

Current school board members get nervous as they anticipate a possible change—whether potentially positive or negative. Nonincumbent candidates may be attacking the district, the board members, or the superintendent, hoping this strategy will get them elected. You need to be focused, strong, and calm for everyone throughout these times.

Key Actions

- Prepare clear and concise materials and messages about the district and distribute to all board candidates
- Plan and hold a workshop for all board candidates, and involve appropriate staff members
- Work with the current board to determine how, or whether, they will participate in the workshop
- Review election guidelines and legal information with staff
- Educate (thoroughly and carefully) administrative staff on the politics of the election
- Serve as a resource to staff should they have questions about the election
- Offer to meet with candidates individually and provide indentical information to each one
- Think about how you will handle challenging election issues
- Use discretion in dealing with the press, who may ask you about the candidates or the election, keeping in mind you work for whomever is elected
- Plan for possible changes in board membership

Almost immediately as a new superintendent, I faced a board election. Fortunately, an experienced superintendent told me that the job of the superintendent in working with a board starts with candidate training before the election.

Following this advice, I developed information sessions for candidates, as well as for current board members who were running for reelection. As I became somewhat familiar with the candidates, my fledgling assumptions as a superintendent were overturned, and a new reality set in. I had naively assumed (hoped) that only people with good intentions would run for the school board and that voters would assess whether candidates had personal/political agendas or really cared about children. I had to confront the reality that logic would not necessarily prevail and the possibility that things might not turn out for the best.

Showing Up

> . . . in less than one year I established a reputation as a superintendent who likes to visit classrooms, who comes to special events during the day and in the evenings and on the weekends.
>
> This commitment to showing up has also caused me some challenges. I was ill one evening and missed an open house at an elementary school. The next day I got a call from the principal asking me if I was mad at him.
>
> —Johnston et al., 2002, p. 64

September and October provide great opportunities for you to be visible. At back-to-school nights, opening day luncheons, and school visits, you have the chance to be seen supporting what matters most-teaching and learning.

Your presence at the back-to-school nights signals the importance of parents as partners. Your classroom visits convey how much you value teachers and students. An appearance at a sporting event, play, or musical performance acknowledges the role of well-rounded experiences for students. These symbolic actions go a long way in communicating what you believe and value. All of these efforts also give you the chance to see and "feel" how things are going. We tend, as educational leaders, to have an intuitive sense about the environment in classes and on school campuses.

Key Actions

- Participate in welcome-back events
- Schedule community presentations with consistent messages related to the new school year

- Thank publicly and privately those who organized all opening activities
- Develop your school site and department visitation schedule
- Communicate your expectations for the school site and department visits (e.g., visit classes, discuss goals, review data)
- Review back-to-school night activities, inviting board, superintendent, and district office staff participation
- Make an initial assessment of how your leadership team is following through on the vision and direction of the district

Speaking From Experience

This is an exciting and exhilarating time of the year. Unlike most private sector businesses, schools have their own unique beginning and end, with a fresh start each fall. As superintendent you send powerful messages about the district through every communication and every symbolic action you take. Take hold of this great opportunity and enjoy the kick-off to another great year.

Upon Reflection

My leadership actions for September and October will be . . .

Building relationships _____
_____
_____

Planning/implementing _____
_____
_____

Communicating _____
_____
_____

Monitoring/revising _____
_____
_____

Coaching/mentoring _____
_____
_____

4

November and December

Checking In and Celebrating Progress

Boards and superintendents who treat each other with respect and have common goals for students demonstrate to the community a true sense of teamwork.

—Johnston et al., 2002

There is no more uplifting profession that being an educational leader. When a superintendent and board have developed a deep and trusting relationship, the students benefit from an organization focused on them. For the superintendent, a positive relationship with the board of education is absolutely critical. Whether a new or a seasoned veteran, an effective superintendent knows that building a solid board relationship is a top priority and a continuous process.

While ongoing communication is a daily effort, certain times of the year create new challenges for superintendents. Whether building a new team after an election, monitoring the budget, assessing facility needs, or closely monitoring programs and student achievement data, you and the board need to model through every action that student learning is your highest priority.

Solidifying Board Relationships

Superintendents know that a change of only one board member can take you back to zero—and it is necessary to create a completely new team. School board elections often bring many challenges, and an important aspect of your job is to review with staff the board election process, guide the staff in the board orientation procedure, and develop a plan for informing new board members regarding all aspects of district operations.

Key Actions

- Develop a survey for new members regarding interests, goals, and focus areas for their board service so you have a written record of this data
- Spend time with individual board members to learn their personal goals and aspirations for their board service
- Establish agreements with board members regarding the most effective way to communicate with each of them
- Spend ample time with each new member providing detailed orientation materials and an opportunity for them to ask questions to help them to understand all aspects of the district's operation
- Continue to educate them throughout their board tenure
- Schedule one-on-one board member meetings in advance of the annual organizational meeting
- Schedule pre-conferences prior to board meetings for new and current board members to ensure they have adequate preparation for agenda issues, particularly current challenges so they are fully prepared and never surprised
- Be proactive and make contact with new board members every week

Building Positive Board Communication

The wise superintendent knows that relationship building never ends. Clear and complete systems of communication contribute to the development of a strong superintendent and board governance team.

> I am an early riser and I love nothing more than to meet with colleagues and board members for an early morning breakfast to brainstorm how to address current challenges when we are all wide awake and energized to start our days.
>
> When I left one superintendency and joined a new district with a much different protocol, I discovered that my predecessor had a much different internal clock than I. He arrived at 9:00 to 9:30 a.m. and had developed a "lunching culture" with board members that had existed for years. I realized my comfortable "breakfast with the board" protocol would require me to do some shifting of my day. At first, I thought I surely could get them to adapt, but I realized it was I who needed to do the shifting. The long lunches once a month have become very valuable slots of time. Not only have we developed a strong understanding of each other's perspectives on district issues, but I also have a more thorough knowledge of their personal histories, their experiences in the district, and their families. As a result, our relationships were cemented very early in my tenure as the superintendent.

A strong, clear plan of coordinated communication activities with the board is critical to a successful and dynamic relationship. Frequent communication with each board member must be prioritized as your essential work.

Key Actions

- Develop a system to document and record interests, goals, questions, and requests for information to ensure a running record of board communication
- Write a detailed memo to yourself titled "Board Members' Interests"; update and refer to it frequently
- Treat all board members alike and provide the same information requested by one to all
- Introduce and put board members out front in meetings with constituents and groups
- Facilitate collaborative relationships among all board members; acknowledge individual strengths and contributions to the board as a collective body
- Celebrate the board and superintendent partnership with retreats and social events that focus on building relationships leading to more effective work on behalf of students
- If your board relationship is not working effectively, take proactive measures to seek support and guidance from a trusted colleague, your professional organization, or consultants who specialize in board/superintendent relationships

Monitoring the Current Budget

The creation of a comprehensive budget document is no easy task. It is essential that you publicly acknowledge the key individuals who play important roles in the budget development process. Because school district revenues and expenditures are subject to constant change, you and your board members must regularly communicate that the budget is a living document and that you monitor it throughout the school year.

The entire organization gains confidence and trust in you as a leader when you develop the ability and skill to effectively communicate the status of the district's budget. When there is ongoing monitoring and communication in strong fiscal years, there is greater trust when the inevitable economic downturns happen.

Key Actions

- Review the budget early in the current year and develop a communication plan to share with constituent groups
- Engage district personnel or the finance committee in proactive planning while monitoring the current year's budget status
- Review budget guidelines and protocols to determine needs and make modifications
- Communicate budget status with existing district and/or community budget advisory committees
- Develop tasks for appropriate budget committees
- Obtain financial and business operations updates and advisories from professional organizations
- Offer your time to communicate the message to community groups
- Develop and use a consistent, jargon-free, user-friendly, one-page budget document which provides a clear picture of the current status of the budget

Monitoring Programs and Student Achievement Data

The district's vision, mission, goals, strategies, policies, and major activities must encourage, promote, and support the key focus of our schools: teaching and learning. You are responsible for guiding an ongoing process that focuses on achievement for every student.

During board meetings there is often time set aside for public acknowledgment of the contributions by various groups. Not coincidentally, school districts with strong track records of student performance are districts in which board agendas reflect ongoing participation and acknowledgment of important contributors to the school system. You can make a difference in the perception outsiders have of your district when you recognize important contributions of various persons. You might ask board members to make presentations to retirees, long-term employees, leaders of food drives, championship athletic and academic teams, and mock trial and essay contest winners. Consider recognizing athletic booster organizations, business partners, county offices of education, coordinating councils, and religious organizations. An expansive array of presentations to a wide range of participants symbolically reflects your and the board's deep appreciation for wide involvement in the important work in the district.

Key Actions

- Schedule quarterly and mid-year meetings and retreats for administration and the board to review goals and accomplishments
- Review all student performance data to determine high priority curricular needs
- Schedule site-by-site meetings with principals to provide an in-depth overview of student performance data and assist them in developing action plans in response to needs
- Design a system where appropriate persons review and document accomplishments related to instructional programs
- Develop annual school performance reports for wide distribution
- Review the curriculum development process
- Review and approve needed course catalog and curriculum revisions
- Review extra- and co-curricular programs

Assessing Facility Needs

You are responsible for having a district facilities master plan to serve as a guide for determining facility needs and concerns. Given the dynamics of potential changes in local community development as well as desired program improvement efforts, a comprehensive plan will provide a blueprint for future planning.

This master strategic plan for facilities must be comprehensive and include all data necessary for decision making, including past and projected enrollment increases and decreases, needs for new construction, and modernization needs for current sites. Demographic shifts can impact district boundaries or require creative ways to address enrollment imbalances in schools, and these must be considered based on the local culture and political context.

A key component of the facilities plan is a comprehensive outline of all available fiscal resources and approaches for the board to consider for facility improvements. In collaboration with local agencies, developers, and members of the community, make an ongoing assessment to ensure the effective delivery of high quality educational programs in facilities that support learning. You may decide the scope of facilities needs and accompanying action plans are so complex that your district personnel are unable to take on all of these tasks. There are professional organizations that can offer suggestions and references for obtaining highly skilled consultants to address district needs.

Key Actions

- Engage the board and all construction, facilities, maintenance and operations, and site-based staff members in identifying and recommending facility needs
- Work with business and fiscal service personnel or consultants in identifying and defining all funding source options
- Develop estimates of costs for meeting each facility's needs
- Estimate the amount of money available from each funding source
- Create an implementation plan that establishes a schedule to obtain funding from the selected sources and then ensure that funds are spent in time to make certain that work is completed to meet identified needs
- Track, adjust, and communicate actions to allow for ever-changing conditions

Speaking From Experience

While the board acts as one body in a public meeting, board members are clearly unique individuals with their own goals and beliefs about education. How the superintendent acknowledges these individuals' strengths sends a powerful message to the community. Inevitably, challenges with budget, program monitoring, and facility needs can cause highs and lows, twists and turns, but successful problem solving evolves when boards and superintendents develop a true commitment to teamwork.

Upon Reflection

My leadership actions for November and December will be . . .

Building relationships _____

_____

_____

Planning/implementing _____

_____

_____

Communicating _____

_____

_____

Monitoring/revising _____

_____

_____

Coaching/mentoring _____

_____

_____

5

January and February

Taking Stock and Planning for Next Year

Keep your organization's time zones in perspective. Honor the past, be cognizant of present priorities, and share a clear vision of the future.

—Johnston et al., 2002

January and February is the time to review the first part of the year, celebrate success, progress toward district goals and priorities, acknowledge problem areas, reprioritize if necessary, and begin some serious planning for the next year. No one person has more access to information or a clearer view of a school system than you, the superintendent. Despite the crush of day-to-day district operations, you must stay focused on the goals of the district supported by a strong mission statement, specific goals, and a system for prioritizing strategies. This system is often referred to as a strategic or long-range plan and is a living document. Keeping the strategic plan alive and meaningful requires that key stakeholders review and update it on a regular basis.

Key focus areas for your consideration during the planning include an assessment of the district's financial stability through the budget process and an ongoing review of the curriculum and instructional focus in the district's classrooms. District goals, strategies, policies, and major activities must encourage, promote, and support excellence in teaching and learning throughout the district and in every school.

Developing a Long-Range Plan

Constancy of purpose is critical for the long-term positive direction of a school and district. Too often we move from one initiative to another without connecting our actions to the whole, losing the constancy and sense by others that we have a common purpose. To set the stage for a formal district strategic planning process, you must develop a personal calendar planning system.

> In my early administrative training programs, I was required to keep a day-by-day log of activities and actions with personal reflections of what had transpired. Because I've continued to keep such a log throughout my career, I have a twenty-year set of journals chronicling the month-by-month routine tasks and unanticipated challenges that have occurred in my career. By revisiting these journals periodically, I have reminders of events that I would easily have forgotten. I have found that these valuable historical documents allow me to reflect on the past and maintain thoughtful perceptions into my current job.

Strategic planning is a valuable, more formal way to focus the organization and is often cited as the CEO's most effective method of moving an organization forward. In a public school district with an elected board of education, you are charged with carrying out this function and ensuring that the organization remains on the course set by the board-approved strategic plan. While there are various models, all involve your spending concentrated time with representatives of groups who care deeply about student learning and who will work to set a clear direction based on shared beliefs. Once mission, vision, beliefs, and goal statements are established, you must be certain they are consistently articulated and shared.

Key Actions

- Gather information from trusted colleagues and professional organizations who can provide materials and insight regarding various approaches to the strategic planning process
- Determine the needs of the organization by creating a planning process that matches the unique needs of your district
- Outline the process and format, noting timelines and including individuals and groups in the goal-setting efforts so there is a clear understanding of the various steps that will be taken to complete the plan
- Develop an organizational chart that communicates the message about institutional priorities and relationships to interested groups
- Print the completed strategic planning outcomes on visual documents that can be posted and shared through various communication links and venues
- Review strategic plan progress and accomplishments on an ongoing basis and establish revised priorities and "course corrections" as needed

Budget Forecasting for the Next Year

A solid foundation of fiscal stability is essential to achieve the core mission of providing a successful instructional program. In order to assist in future planning you must make a thorough assessment of the fiscal state of the district. Clearly and openly communicating the district's budget makes what can be a complex and confusing process understandable. By making sure you have a dedicated and sharp focus on the budget planning process as the planning begins for a new year, you and the board will reap enormous benefits and credibility. Creating a solid budget will assure the resources to support and implement dynamic instructional programs that will move the district forward educationally. Frequently communicate budget stability and continued commitment to instructional enhancements that increase student performance. This will assure your community that you and the board are focused on developing the next generation of leaders.

Key Actions

- Interpret state budget projections and the impact on the district
- Attend workshops designed to provide guidelines to districts regarding new budget initiatives
- Finalize the district budget planning master calendar for board approval
- Design a budget communication document that explains complex information in an easily understood format
- Schedule board retreats and study sessions to review the budget for coming year
- Develop "road show" presentations throughout the community to address budget issues for appropriate constituent groups
- Tie the budget to the district's long-range or strategic plan

Reviewing the Curriculum and Establishing Goals

The success of each student is the responsibility of the superintendent. While a large group of administrators, teachers, and support personnel deliver instruction in an array of settings in the district, ultimately you are accountable for providing the finest educational program that can be envisioned.

> While visiting classrooms I always ask principals and staff members how I can help them do their jobs better. The most common response is to keep coming back to observe them at work. These informal visits yield rich data about the curriculum and how it is being delivered, the teacher's style, and the interest and enthusiasm of the students. I walk through the classrooms and talk with principals. This gives me an opportunity to discuss how the principal is coaching and assessing the professional development of the staff. We talk about leadership activities and challenges, the budget, the facilities, and any factors that influence the daily life of the school. These visits provide me with opportunities to gauge progress and learn about potential new focus areas for the coming year.

When you work toward systematic curriculum development and staff development programs, you will move the district forward. Provide comprehensive student assessment data to the principals, grade-level teams, and individual teachers, along with support for interpretation and guidance regarding program improvement. One of your highest priorities is to deliberately establish high expectations, provide needed resources, and to monitor and review what's happening in each classroom. This is a team effort, and you, the superintendent, are the leader of the team—communicating expectations, providing resources, and having a consistent organizational system, focused on academic success for all students.

Key Actions

- Develop a master responsibility chart to outline the department leaders who have responsibility for each curriculum area
- Develop month-by-month lists of specific tasks and focus areas that the educational services leadership team is responsible for accomplishing
- Survey staff development needs for all school sites to determine multi-year needs for training support for employees
- Review curriculum material and the textbook adoption cycle
- Prioritize the curricular areas to be addressed during coming school year
- Institute student assessment programs in all content areas to provide longitudinal data on student performance
- Compile detailed data documents individualized by school, grade level, content area, and student in order to develop instructional support programs for each student in the system
- Monitor school site plans and assist sites in documenting accomplishments
- Develop action plans for summer school program implementation
- Review responsibilities and accomplishments of established councils, committees, or advisory groups related to curriculum development and goal setting
- Develop the structure for communication of annual student performance data
- Expand efforts to celebrate staff achievements and professionalism

Communicating New Focus Areas and Priorities

As superintendent, you must frequently ask whether the organization can inspire even more opportunities in your schools that will result in greater accomplishments for students. Through regular monitoring, presentations at board meetings on district initiatives, and reports on student performance, you and the board demonstrate that progress toward reaching district goals is a priority. Administrators and teachers are asked to continually assess student achievement targets and goals at their schools. You and the board need to model the same behavior. When gaps arise between our goals and our results, new focus areas and priorities evolve and become part of the strategic plan for the coming year. Continually ask yourself if you are on track or if there is more you can do. These are important reflections for you and the board as leaders.

Key Actions

- Develop a culture of inquiry by asking questions including: Are we achieving our goals? What do we need to improve? How can we do better? Are we reaching every student?
- Document accomplishments on a monthly basis and add a correlated list of new areas of focus that have emerged by grade level and department, by school site, and by district department
- Set specific dates in the calendar year to review and revise the long-range plan with new areas of focus for board consideration and approval
- Celebrate and widely share accomplishments and announce with great fanfare new initiatives focused on student support

Sharing the State of the District

As the new calendar year begins, you will find it is a perfect time to share highlights from every area of district operations with the wider community.

At the beginning of my first year as superintendent, I shared four themes with my leadership team: Improved Student Learning, Caring, Commitment, and Efficiency and Effectiveness. I described each one and gave specific examples from their schools that exemplified the themes at a high level. At the beginning of my second year at the leadership team kick-off gathering, I started by putting on the big screen the themes from our first year together. Then I told everyone I would share the themes for the coming year. When the SAME four themes appeared on the screen, the result was laughter and applause. My explanation for the same four themes was that what we stand for does not change. Our methods to achieve our goals may change, but our commitment to principles does not change.

You can generate enthusiasm by staging a mid-year celebratory communication process related to the strategic plan and new focus areas that are driving our work. Students are our primary constituent group. Through your highlighting of major events, progress toward goals and priorities, and challenges and plans for the future, you keep the entire community "in the know." In so doing, you enhance your district's credibility and the public's confidence in the educational system.

Key Actions

- Identify all "publics" and constituencies that would value information about the vision, goals, accomplishments, and critical issues facing the district
- Create a calendar of speaking engagements with the numerous groups that represent your key community leaders
- Prepare a board briefing on the "State of the District" and present it at board meetings, school sites, and district departmental meetings
- Begin planning and gathering information for an expanded version of the "State of the District" for the board/superintendent mid-year retreat
- Publish the "State of the District" in a communitywide newsletter
- Write an article about the district's accomplishments for email distribution, local newspapers, school newsletters, and the district's Web site

Speaking From Experience

At the beginning of the calendar year, which coincides with the midpoint of an academic year in our schools, you take stock of the progress the district is making. Your role is always challenging and often daunting, and there can be a tendency to dwell on the negative, difficult, and distressing aspects of the job when, in fact, you have far more joyous moments to celebrate if you take the time to quietly reflect. To prepare for the year and the host of opportunities it brings, start with a renewed, refreshed attitude and perspective and new ideas to stretch your budgets, communicate your priorities, and share the accomplishments. As difficult as the job can be, there is nothing better than being able to be a significant force in a child's life, and that is what needs to be remembered during these months.

Upon Reflection

My leadership actions for January and February will be . . .

Building relationships _____
_____
_____

Planning/implementing _____
_____
_____

Communicating _____
_____
_____

Monitoring/revising _____
_____
_____

Coaching/mentoring _____
_____
_____

6

March and April

Staying Focused and Facing Challenges

Evident in the tone of almost all the personal-best stories is that leaders are people who seize the initiative with enthusiasm, determination, and a desire to make something happen.

—Kouzes & Posner, 2007

March and April bring complexity, challenging a leader's skills and ability to stay focused. This is the period when, as superintendent, you must have the whole district pictured in your head.

At this very busy time of the year, as you interact with various stakeholders, consider how the decisions you make will impact progress toward the district's vision for all learners. Stay calm with a laser-like focus while you make key decisions concerning educational programs, human resources, and the budget. This will allow you to continue to move the district toward meeting the goals and objectives outlined in the strategic plan. Build on your prior planning and collaboration and continue to ask district office leaders and principals clarifying questions that will assist them in effectively managing the changes you have laid out for the future.

Budget Planning

When his district faced budget challenges that required making significant cuts, the superintendent knew he needed a clear plan for addressing issues. He knew it was critical to develop two key sets of data. First, he and the board had to agree on the creation of a budget development calendar that described every required action with an associated timeline. The superintendent also recognized that essential to the yearly budget development process was the adoption of a set of guidelines for decision making. He had his district staff develop and present a template of proposed budget guidelines for the board to review. By communicating the process and timeline, the superintendent and board provided a transparent plan so all stakeholders could understand and know when and how they could participate.

—Townsend et al., 2006, p. 69

The budget represents the district's priorities expressed in numbers. All stakeholders need constant reminders that although the budget planning process often proceeds at the same time as program planning, it does not supersede program planning.

A critical responsibility of the business official is to provide current budget information as well as up-to-date budget projections. The business leader needs to provide continuous information regarding potential legislative impacts and economic factors.

During this period, it is your responsibility to keep the board, staff, and community focused on the district's role as an institution whose primary mission is supporting teaching and learning. As the budget is prepared, the superintendent's role can be compared to that of the symphony conductor who keeps the entire orchestra working together to perform a harmonious and beautiful piece of music.

Key Actions

- Review three-year budget and expenditure histories for patterns
- Review current year expenditures by program for budget and expense alignment
- Meet with the finance committee to review their recommendations to the board
- Formulate budget goals and assumptions for the next year
- Compile budget requests from department heads and principals

- Review finance committee recommendations and district staff requests with the board
- Determine the board's priorities for meeting student needs
- Review the tentative budget with cabinet members
- Review additions and corrections to the new budget document with division managers
- Review budget adoption timelines with the board for the next school year

Planning for Facility Upgrades

In addition to planning the overall budget, the business division needs your help and guidance as they plan and prepare schools for the work that will be completed during summer recess. Consider all of the information from principals about the critical needs and desired improvements at their schools in accordance with the facilities master plan and the funds available for capital projects for the new fiscal year. Reassure a principal who finds a long awaited project has been delayed; give the reason and a revised projected timeline for completing the work. The specifics will help the principal explain the situation to the staff and community.

Key Actions

- Meet with the business division staff to determine the status of summer facilities improvement projects
- Review the status of the five-year facilities master plan with the board
- Place bids and quotes for capital projects on the board agenda for review and approval
- Set priorities for facilities upgrades
- Communicate priorities and timelines to staff and community
- Determine the status of projects that face delays
- Work with the business division to develop alternate timelines when projects are re-bid or delayed
- Provide a reason and new timeline for principals when projects at their schools are delayed

Targeting Personnel Actions

Sometimes in this job you can get overwhelmed and wonder why you ever wanted to be a superintendent. However, just find one "Bill" for a new principalship and you know exactly why. . . . In his second year, I see tremendous positive changes in the school. He is still smiling. The staff and students love him. His smile is tinged with more wisdom and confidence. Every day I know I made the right choice. His commitment and desire to do a great job have been a joy to watch.

—Johnston et al., 2002, pp. 70–71

By this time of the year you and the staff have made non-reemployment decisions, delivered layoff notices, and held meetings with the affected staff. Retirees have notified human resources of their plans to leave at the end of the school year. Recruitment teams are working and beginning to make their recommendations for hiring new personnel.

Human resources staff meet with each administrator to finalize, as much as possible, staffing for each school. They also determine if any extra recruiting efforts are necessary to fill difficult positions in such areas as math, science, special education, and English learner classes. A level of ambiguity exists, because for the next few months, some teachers may decide to leave the district for any number of reasons and opt out of their contracts.

Enrollment may decline or increase slightly or dramatically. Your job is to ensure that human resources and business staff work together closely to coordinate an effective position control system. As superintendent, you are finalizing plans to promote, hire, or transfer school- or district-level administrators and completing timelines to fill vacant leadership positions. Invaluable at this time is a comprehensive human resources calendar for you and the board that includes all major timelines. The human resources staff needs comprehensive timelines for all their internal decisions.

Key Actions

- Prepare for board action on non-reelection of certificated and classified personnel
- Ensure that layoff notices are board approved and delivered on time and with sensitivity

- Meet with union leaders regarding layoffs that affect members of their associations
- Meet with human resources staff to determine the status of recruitment efforts
- Prepare board agenda items if additional recruitment trips require approval
- Meet with business and human resources division leaders to ensure coordination of budget details, personnel needs, and requests
- Develop plans for filling vacant administrative positions, promotions, or transfers

Monitoring Curriculum, Instruction, and Student Testing Plans

March and April are busy periods for the human resources and business divisions. Their activities command a fair share of your attention because critical personnel, budget, and facilities decisions for the next year are made during these months.

Curriculum and instruction leaders are also working with principals on plans to prepare for the annual state testing program, summer school programs, summer inservice, and identifying new/required curriculum development projects. Additionally, they are submitting new course offerings and textbook adoption recommendations to you for board approval. Once again, a curriculum instruction and assessment calendar of key timelines can ensure major work is kept on track.

Ask the important questions of the educational services staff about how the budget for inservice and curriculum development is aligned with the staff's needs for skill development. The foundation for the assessment of staff needs should be the analysis of multiple measures of student achievement and responses to implementing new state mandates. Determine if the plans are consistent with the district's goals and that the principals' plans for implementation are in place.

A wise superintendent asks questions about the preparedness of the system to ensure that teachers and students will have the classroom materials they require. Failure of the system to have adequate books and materials for the opening of school can lead to embarrassing questions for you and the board at the first meeting of the coming school year. Worse, it means instructional time is lost.

Key Actions

- Meet with the leaders of the curriculum and instruction unit to plan for summer school, summer inservice, and new or revised curriculum projects
- Place new course plans and textbook adoption recommendations on the board agenda for approval and public review
- Review the business division's status with respect to ordering, processing, and delivering instructional materials and equipment for the new school year
- Review the assessment/evaluation department's plans for assisting schools with the state testing programs
- Send a letter to parents emphasizing the importance of state testing programs and solicit their cooperation and support

Planning Board and Leadership Team Workshops/Retreats/Advances

The school board and the leadership team must be at the forefront of supporting continuous improvement and renewal for themselves and the entire district staff. The value of the annual beginning-of-the-school-year board and administrative team workshops/retreats cannot be underestimated. It is during these meetings that you set the tone for the entire school year. People tend to be at high levels of energy and hope for the new school year. Take advantage of this optimistic spirit by carefully planning these events. The content of these meetings is the result of your discussions with the board and your leadership team regarding the district's strategic plan, evaluations from previous retreats, and new state mandates.

The board–superintendent workshop/retreat does not usually involve the district staff; however, board members often are invited to join the leadership team retreat, particularly the opening session. Principals and other leaders need to know the general theme(s) for the year and the board and superintendent's expectations for the coming school year. Work with the team to have cohesion with themes, activities, and speakers.

Plan your own professional development for the year. Ensure "your" time is on your calendar and included in the budget. Attendance at state and national educational conferences and workshops not only keeps you current in your profession and inspires continuous improvement, it also gives you the opportunity to share experience and expertise with colleagues.

Key Actions

- Determine important topics/issues to explore during the board workshop/retreat/advance; share suggestions with the board
- Select the workshop/retreat planning team and provide it with budget parameters
- Ensure the planning team matches the suitability of a consultant(s) based on identified needs of the group before engaging services
- Ensure a venue is selected that will enhance outcomes and is within budget
- Ensure the planning team builds in an appropriate evaluation of the workshop/retreat and has a plan for rapid turnaround of results
- Plan a social occasion to include all leadership team members, their guests, and the board; if you have space, host the event in your home
- Establish your own professional development plan for the year

Beginning Evaluations of the Administrative Staff

Positions that are in direct line for you to evaluate vary by size of district, by board policy, and by past practice. The evaluation process allows you to determine how well an administrator is contributing to the accomplishment of the district's vision, mission, and goals, and the extent to which the individual has met a set of previously agreed upon goals and objectives. In recent years the evaluation process for administrators is tied to state standards for administrators or standards developed by the various professional associations unique to particular administrative functions.

Whatever process or instrument used, provide sufficient feedback on the administrator's performance to ensure continuous improvement and growth of the individual as well the school, department, or division the employee leads. It is a natural opportunity for you to mentor and coach leaders to increase their skills and discuss future leadership plans.

Develop a calendar of meetings with your administrators to ensure you set evaluation expectations with them prior to the beginning of the year. The evaluation calendar also includes periodic monitoring of progress and the date for completion of the annual written assessment. While the calendar is important for those you evaluate, it is invaluable for keeping you on track.

Key Actions

- Schedule sufficient time to meet with each administrator you evaluate
- Establish an annual calendar for evaluations
- Require administrators to provide written documents regarding their contribution to the district's vision, mission, and goals; their personal goals and objectives; and, if appropriate, documents reflecting their accomplishments relative to state or other standards for administrators at least two weeks in advance of your scheduled evaluation conference
- Prepare a draft evaluation based on your document review and personal observations
- Review the evaluation with the administrator and seek further input
- Modify final evaluation documents for the administrator's signature

Speaking From Experience

In most school districts across the country, the months of March and April are filled with tension around "high stakes testing." These are the months when students take state and federal achievement tests used to determine whether schools have met student achievement targets. The results have a significant impact on the districts' reputation and standing in the community, state, and nation. In many cases, these test results impact whether the districts will be identified under the federal No Child Left Behind Act as "low performing or program improvement school districts."

The pre-testing period is an especially important time for you to visit schools and classrooms and assure administrators, teachers, and students that you understand the pressure they are feeling. Remind them of your support and respect for all of their hard work during the past several months to be prepared for these important measures of student learning. Have lunch with school staff and be a morale booster and cheerleader. They especially need your encouragement and energy at this time of the year.

Upon Reflection

My leadership actions for March and April will be . . .

Building relationships _____

_____

_____

Planning/implementing _____

_____

_____

Communicating _____

_____

_____

Monitoring/revising _____

_____

_____

Coaching/mentoring _____

_____

_____

7

May and June

Wrapping Up and Celebrating

Despite the crush of day-to-day district operations, superintendents must stay focused on the goals of the district.

—Townsend et al., 2006

Basketball fanatics look forward all year to March Madness—the NCAA Tournament in which virtually every game from the round of 64 to the national title game reaches a fevered pitch.

School districts have their own version of March Madness (even though it is in May and June)—an exciting, exhilarating, sometimes exasperating time of year filled with the anticipation of and planning for critical tasks and end-of-the-year events and celebrations. Emotions tend to run higher, and even celebrations are fraught with anxiety: the senior who won't know until the last minute if he will walk at graduation, even though relatives have flown in from around the country; the first year teacher who wonders if enrollment will warrant having her position again the next fall; the board, anxious to learn the final resource allocations from the city or state in order to make budget adjustments.

Even though superintendents are challenged on multiple fronts, it is time for you to step up and acknowledge the tension—both good and bad—and remind everyone to be extra thoughtful of each other. Students, parents, staff, and board members benefit from "naming" what is going on, and knowing that it is normal as the year winds down. The "gentleness and kindness" message is a reminder to one's self of the power of modeling extra vigilance in how we deal with everyone we encounter—even those whose emotions have run amok.

Adopting the Budget

While you may not have all the data to make a fully informed, definitive budget recommendation, the board has to adopt a budget for the coming year. You have to use the best available information, and the board has to act. Open communication with all stakeholders from the beginning to the end of the process is critical.

Key Actions

- Complete and update all budget assumptions and projections
- Share the proposed budget with the leadership team, union leaders, all staff or staff representatives, parents, and the media
- Ensure public input is communicated to staff and the board
- Provide an additional budget workshop if anything unusual has occurred with assumptions, projections, or allocations
- Make sure the budget is approved on time

Reviewing New Staff Hiring

Since 80 percent plus of a typical district budget is personnel, tasks surrounding staffing are critical, and your decisions will make or break the budget process. The positions of current staff may be affected, and they need to know where they stand; union leaders will want to know how the budget affects the members of their organization. To get the best new staff, you want to interview and select candidates as soon as possible.

Key Actions

- Review the latest enrollment projections

- Communicate changes to the board immediately
- Keep school sites and union leaders aware of all actions, as well as potential future adjustments
- Determine the interview process and timeline, and identify who will participate on the interview team for various positions
- Interview all administrative finalists; in smaller districts you may interview all teaching finalists
- Ensure re-employment of staff, i.e., renewal of administrative contracts
- Ensure the board takes action on all new hires
- Communicate/publicize broadly the names of new hires

Evaluating the Superintendent

The superintendent evaluation, including an annual discussion session with a written evaluation, is critical for you, the board, and the direction of the district.

It is not uncommon for the superintendent evaluation to "slip." This is a problem! If your contract does not include an annual written evaluation, amend the contract. The reasons are important: to be sure you and the board are headed in the same direction, the goals are clear, and any concerns are addressed. Accountability comes from the top. The board and superintendent must model what you want to see in the district and that continuous improvement is a high value for everyone in the organization.

Key Actions

- Provide the board with copies of the evaluation instrument and timelines
- Provide the board with data and narrative on the accomplishments—or lack of—of the year's goals prior to the meeting
- Offer to respond to any individual board member's questions prior to the evaluation meeting
- Include proposed goals for the coming year in your documentation for the board's consideration, as well as areas you believe you need to address regarding your performance
- Send the board a copy of the board–superintendent protocols; part of the superintendent's review should be a board self-review of its adherence to the agreed upon operating procedures; if

protocols do not exist, recommend a goal for the next year to establish these

- Schedule enough time for a thorough, thoughtful discussion
- Recommend having an outside consultant facilitate the review session to allow you and all board members to participate fully and to keep the session on target through completion
- Have the facilitator perform several important tasks, including assisting the board with discussions, mediating differences of opinion to bring the board to consensus on direction for the future, and the difficult work of writing the evaluation draft for the board's review
- Ensure the board completes the evaluation in writing and announces the results of its evaluation; in addition to meeting their contractual responsibilities, announcing the completion of the evaluation demonstrates the board's commitment to performance reviews and accountability
- Address any potential changes to your employment contract; a facilitator can help with this since it can be difficult to negotiate one's own contract
- Have the board extend your contract upon a satisfactory (or excellent!) review and announce it at the meeting and in a press release; this is an opportunity for the board to recognize the work you are doing and let the staff and public know they support you and the direction of the district
- Set goals and/or focus areas for the coming year and write this into the evaluation as part of the next year's performance review
- Have every board member sign the evaluation; in the case of a split opinion, the board president will sign
- Have the facilitator prepare a letter of recommendation signed by all board members based on the evaluation; the letter goes in your personnel file—you never know when it will be useful
- Consider with the board if there is a better time of year to do your annual review; perhaps after major student data information is available is a better time than the end of the school year

Debriefing With Board Members

Every board member has goals and wishes. Board meetings do not provide the setting for open dialog with the full board, nor for individual members. It is not the place for musing about the district; a private, debriefing meeting is such a setting. This being said, it is important that you find appropriate times to get to know individual board members and to understand their goals and wishes.

Key Actions

- Spend quality time with each individual board member
- Ask for their thoughts and insights about the goals and direction of the district
- Consider a breakfast or lunch meeting for a more casual setting; take each member to the same location to avoid concerns of favoritism
- Keep a record of their thoughts and ideas and how you might address them, or if you should

Scheduling Attendance at Year-End Events for You and the Board Members

Symbolic leadership means being visible and showing that you and the board members value the work and achievements of the students and staff. People are proud of what they have accomplished, and year-end events are a way for you to see what they have done and acknowledge and validate their work.

Key Actions

- Make sure you have every important date on your calendar
- Make sure all board members have a complete schedule of year-end events well in advance
- If you and/or a board member is going to speak at an event, be sure you know the theme, amount of allotted time, where to sit, and any other expectations or requests
- When there are conflicts in dates for events, develop a plan for board member attendance at each event so no school is left out
- Do the same regarding coverage of events by you and your senior administrative leaders

Planning Time for Handling Difficult Issues

When deadlines—lots of them—come due, issues arise. Plan on it! Set aside blocks of time to handle tough things—upset parents, teachers, and students. These are high-stakes times—i.e., graduation, testing, promotions, and staffing changes. Time is a precious resource and it is difficult to set aside a block of time, but difficult issues demand time, so try to create space for dealing with thorny concerns. Remember this is all part of our end-of-the-year March Madness.

Key Actions

- Keep open time on your calendar to address a wide variety of difficult issues
- Review policies on graduation requirements and make sure they include a process for who walks and doesn't walk at graduation and how you will deal with parental concerns ensure that the policy is communicated at the beginning of the senior year
- Review procedures on what to say to personnel who want to discuss why they are not being asked back for the following year
- Review processes that teachers can use to communicate concerns about their administrators

Finalizing Summer Activities

Wrapping up one year merges with preparing for the next year. This is what contributes to the "madness." You have to keep an eye on "now" and an eye on "then." People count on you, and that's a good thing.

Key Actions

- Review classroom and building cleaning and repair schedules with maintenance and operations staff
- Monitor field renovations; ensure these have been worked through with city, parks and recreation, boys and girls clubs, and other partners' staff so everyone knows the plan for summer use
- Review professional development activities with instructional staff; ensure activities are in line with district goals and build on prior learning
- Put professional development activities on your calendar and plan to attend several, staying an hour or the entire time, not just dropping in

- Have appropriate staff, including principals, review student discipline policies and prepare recommended improvements
- Ensure business and purchasing staff order time-sensitive items so they arrive for school opening

Finalizing Plans for Next Year's Pre-Opening Activities

Most people start a jigsaw puzzle by doing the border first. It's as if they seem to need some sort of organizational structure. . . . Often the parameters of a problem are defined, but the challenge is in seeing the whole picture. . . . Sometimes there are clues and pieces of information that seem to come together, just as we match colors and shapes in jigsaw puzzles. . . . One needs to simply sit, look closely, take time, rearrange, readjust, step away, step forward, and the pieces will eventually fit together.

—Johnston et al., 2002, pp. 124–125

Just as ending the year well is important, starting the year right is critical. The pre-opening activities with the leadership team, the new staff, and the returning staff set the tone for the year. Your energy and enthusiasm, in addition to your message of goals, themes, and dreams, sets the stage for a year of accomplishments.

Key Actions

- Prepare the list of accomplishments for the current year and plan to highlight and celebrate these as you go into the new school year
- Determine broad themes and goals you will communicate to all stakeholders throughout the coming year
- Begin thinking and planning about the leadership team's retreat (or advance, or convocation, as some districts call them)
- Meet with leaders of parent association groups to gather dates of their major events for the coming year
- Get input from all schools and related community organizations to build a district-wide calendar of events, include board meeting, strategic planning, and other critical committee dates
- Communicate the district calendar broadly

- Have back-to-school nights and other critical school events on your personal calendar
- Make sure all board members have these events on their calendars and encourage them to attend as many as their schedules allow
- Review the calendar regularly and publish updates
- Use the calendar as a basis for developing the next year's calendar; it can be an effective "tickler" file

Reviewing the District Media/ Communication Plan

Communication is the glue that holds all stakeholders together or puts them in separate camps, either fighting each other or eyeing each other with suspicion. Assessing what went right, what went wrong, what was effective, or what was sloppy is important. Trust is built— or lost—on effective communication.

Key Actions

- Review and revise communication documents such as finger tip facts, the Web site, key communicators email list, press releases, etc.
- Meet with local reporter(s) to review upcoming year-end events, inviting coverage
- Learn about new reporters and begin to get to know them
- Ask reporters about deadlines; let them know you will make every effort to call them back to meet a deadline on an important story
- Prepare at least a draft, if not the final, district report for the year; fall is also a good time to release the report

Completing Summative Evaluations of the People Who Report to You

As my first year came to an end, I completed written evaluations. . . . In the evaluation conference . . . I provided comments on the principals' strengths and areas in which I perceived they could do better. While they previously indicated a desire for

feedback, the principals were somewhat stunned by the sugges-
tions for change or improvement. Two of my strongest principals
were amazed about some of my perceptions. It was apparent that
no one had ever suggested areas for improvement to them, even
though many suggestions reflected common views regarding their
leadership. Despite their surprised reactions, the principals appre-
ciated the honest feedback.

For the first time they experienced an evaluation process that
contributed to their professional development. It also gave me an
opportunity to model the quality of the evaluations I expected
they would provide for their own staff members.

—Johnston et al., 2002, p. 72

Just as you need final feedback from your "bosses," so do the people
who report to you. Nothing in the summative evaluation should be a
surprise. Assessment is not an event, but a communication process,
an ongoing dialog about goals, progress, and effectiveness or lack
thereof. The summative evaluation time is a chance to review the
entire year and set new goals just as you set your goals with the board
members.

Key Actions

- Prepare a draft of the summative evaluation using a variety of
  data, including the individual's self-assessment
- Meet with each person to review and discuss the evaluation;
  have a very frank conversation about accomplishments and
  goals for the next year and beyond; this is a collaborative
  process, but you make the final decisions
- Develop an improvement plan with anyone about whom you
  have concerns, laying out specific goals, activities, timelines,
  and means of assessing accomplishment
- For those achieving at a high level, work with them to develop
  next steps as well as a continuous improvement plan—What
  are their aspirations? How can you provide them the opportunities in new areas to prepare for their next position?
- Brief the board on your assessment of leadership personnel
  privately
- Provide a final, written evaluation to each person and give a
  copy to human resources for placement in their files

Preparing the Internal Meeting Calendar for Board and Senior Staff

The work of the senior staff flows from your direction based on board meetings and the critical tasks to be done. Timelines are met when everyone involved makes clear plans around the district priorities.

Key Actions

- Review minutes of the year's board meetings and list routine and special topics for the coming year
- Prepare a rough draft of a 12-month board meeting calendar of major topics by department aligned with district goals
- Send the draft to senior staff and principals to determine potential conflicts with religious holidays, major school events, and professional development days, etc.
- Have senior staff review the year and prepare a draft of their department's 12-month calendar for your review
- Approve senior staff vacation so the district has leadership coverage at all times
- Be sure the board and senior staff know when your vacation is and who will be in charge in your absence

Speaking From Experience

The pace of activities in these months is intense, but YOU cannot be intense—or at least show it. You are the calm, collected leader handling the crush of events and difficult issues while enjoying the fruits of the year's hard work. You are the head cheerleader for the accomplishments of the students and staff. You and the board have the privilege of recognizing and honoring those who have done so much while you are setting your sights on creating the next year's highlights.

Upon Reflection

My leadership actions for May and June will be . . .

Building relationships _____

_____

_____

Planning/implementing _____
_____
_____

Communicating _____
_____
_____

Monitoring/revising _____
_____
_____

Coaching/mentoring _____
_____
_____

8

The Routine and Expected

Communities working collaboratively make differences in the lives of its children and together even the most challenging obstacles can be overcome.

—Johnston et al., 2002

Throughout each school year you are engaged in thousands of leadership conversations. These conversations take place with school district personnel, students, parents, and a wide variety of local and state community members. They focus on building relationships, collaborating, planning, implementing, monitoring, and communicating. Usually they occur through face-to-face, one-on-one meetings in small or large groups, in phone or Web conferences, or via email. You have daily opportunities to become a strong voice for the children and families in their communities, and you have the opportunity to represent their needs in the many ways that emerge.

This chapter reiterates some of the key actions listed in prior chapters in the book. The intention is to highlight for you, all in one place, the "nuts and bolts" of the recurring work of the superintendent that takes place throughout the school year. We suggest that you use this chapter as a "check for detailed planning" as you prepare your annual calendar.

Planning, Leading, and Attending Meetings

A superintendent's workday is frequently an ongoing procession of meetings. During these meetings deep conversations take place. It is where you create visions, generate enthusiasm, collaborate, and make commitments that directly and indirectly impact the quality of teaching and learning for students. While meetings are sometimes referred to in jest as "eating up my day or evening," they are, in fact, where the majority of your work takes place.

The district administrative team is an extension of the superintendent's office, and you must set expectations for their active participation and leadership in district and community committees. This important cabinet team becomes "a family at work." The ups and downs of the jobs and the tears and laughter that emerge are all part of the rhythm of working together to further opportunities for our students.

> *After a meeting at which the teachers' union and classified union conducted an unusually loud and raucous demonstration about their lack of an acceptable salary increase and the singing of a well-known song with lyrics that challenged my leadership ability, the value of our debriefing meeting became especially clear to all of us. At the beginning of the meeting, we glumly reviewed our own personal points of view about the demonstration. As we continued our debriefing, one of the cabinet members quietly expressed her disappointment and jealousy that no one sang a song about her, and suddenly we all burst into laughter. For a few brief minutes we all found ways to relieve the carryover tension of this meeting by considering other songs that could be sung by us at a future meeting.*
>
> —Johnston et al., 2002, p. 57

Meetings that you or board members lead need to have the same kind of detailed attention as lesson plans you prepared when you were in the classroom. You are "on stage" during meetings just like classroom teachers, where everyone is watching you and gauging your level of commitment, knowledge, and expertise. Even when you attend other meetings as a guest, you may be asked to make a comment or give opening remarks. You want to make sure you always have some carefully thought through comments regarding some aspect of the work of the district ready for public presentation even at the most unlikely event. Even when you do not speak, you are being watched, and your behavior sends symbolic messages.

Key Actions

School Board Meetings

- Pre-plan using a 12-month calendar, an agreed-upon template for the agenda, and involve an agenda-planning team
- Pay attention to logistics and prepare for the unexpected
- Carefully design the board packet for each meeting
- Communicate the agenda widely and make sure board members are prepared for the meeting
- Conduct each board meeting as though it is the most important one; at that point it is
- Debrief board meetings with staff and list tasks and assignments

Principals and District Office Staff

- Schedule regular meetings (weekly/biweekly/monthly) and plan each meeting with the outcome in mind and a carefully detailed agenda to support the outcome
- Include participants meaningfully and use their valuable time wisely
- Give participants opportunities to problem solve and share their expertise and suggestions regarding initiatives
- Allow participants time to have their questions answered and respond to rumors and anxieties

Individual District and School Administrators

- Schedule weekly or biweekly meetings to ensure you are up to date regarding school and department issues and concerns
- Review progress toward meeting annual goals and professional development

Campus and Classroom Visits

- Schedule regular meetings to address issues and concerns and collaborate on initiatives
- Review data and progress toward meeting district goals

- Follow up site visits with short emails and notes to staff and site leadership highlighting positive observations

Community Members (City Officials, Elected Officials, Business Leaders, Community Leaders, Other Education Leaders)

- Schedule meetings as needed to address issues and concerns
- Create ways to collaborate on communitywide initiatives
- Share data and progress toward meeting district goals

External Experts and Consultants

- Schedule meetings to ensure you are kept up to date on the status of deliverables and timelines regarding curriculum audits, school construction, professional development, coaching, etc.
- Meet as needed with legal counsel to review school or department issues and new legislation, as well as discuss legal cases that have potential impact for your district

Monitoring for Accountability

Holding yourself and others accountable for accomplishing goals, objectives, and benchmarks is a critical attribute of a successful superintendent.

Schedule regular monitoring and update meetings that coordinate with your calendar and the school district calendar. Most student data should be reviewed monthly and analyzed for trends to prevent surprises, celebrate accomplishments, and adjust strategies. Other data might only need to be reviewed quarterly to ensure that corrections and adjustments can be implemented in a timely manner. Regularly calendar the monitoring of any special projects or new initiatives to ensure that everyone involved knows you are giving this work a high level of attention.

Key Actions

Student Achievement

- Review district formative benchmark scores, attendance, discipline, truancy data, grade point averages, AP and SAT scores, and any other relevant student information

- Meet with principals to discuss progress and/or concerns and plan follow-up action as needed
- Define structure and key dates for completion of site-based school improvement action plans

Budget

- Review monthly income and expenditures and compare to budget projections
- Review student enrollment data
- Review all budget targets and plan follow-up action as needed

Operations and Facilities Master Plan

- Review operations issues, responses, and actions
- Review facilities targets against timelines and budgets and plan follow-up action as needed
- Update plans with established timelines to ensure issues are addressed in a timely manner

Human Resources

- Review position controls, open positions, and hiring status
- Review human resources issues such as grievances, suspensions, and complaints and plan follow-up action as needed

Professional Development

- Review status of ongoing professional development and evaluations from staff
- Review future needs, plans, and budget projections

New Initiative Stakeholder Meetings

- Plan visits to schools; local civic, professional and business groups; and other community-based groups to discuss new initiatives and progress in the school district
- Convene planning or advisory groups that were involved in new initiative development and provide updates on progress

Curriculum Development, Instruction, and Assessment

- Review curriculum work, instruction changes, and progress in meeting benchmarks
- Conduct classroom walkthroughs with administrators (and teachers) to monitor curriculum and instruction improvements

- Review progress in developing school-based and district assessments of student achievement
- Attend grade-level team or department meetings to hear about teacher ideas, collaboration, and response to student learning

Communication Plan

- Review all elements of your communication plan including contacts with board members, administrators, teachers, staff, students, and community
- Update organizational and responsibility charts as needed
- Schedule meetings with media personnel
- Continually assess all emergency planning processes and proactively review and practice all protocols and procedures
- Review guidelines regarding use of site phones, cell phones, and mass calling phone systems for parent communications
- Update district and site Web sites, intranet resources, and electronic communication processes within the district, outside groups, and other agencies

Establishing Relationships and Building Community

Taking the time to establish a positive relationship with your union leadership yields big dividends for the district, especially during tough budget times. Being truthful and open about the budget and talking through difficult issues and conflicts together can build relationships that contribute positively to future contract negotiations and many other employee situations. Having the union perspective is essential to building collaborative plans and meeting goals.

Workdays, evenings, and weekends are frequently filled with school and community events that are important for you to attend. Usually the school district is one of the largest enterprises in the community, and you are expected to be visible as the leader of the organization. These events provide you an opportunity to share the good news about successes at schools and in the district, as well as solicit support for new initiatives. It is also a time for you to build relationships with parents and other members of the community you do not see on a regular basis. Attend as many of these events as you reasonably can to let people know you are not only committed to the school district, but to the community at large.

Key Actions

Union Leaders

- Meet regularly to keep lines of communication and information open and accessible with a focus on interest-based problem-solving approaches
- Share areas of concern and collaborate on strategies to resolve problems
- Provide "heads up" copies of district communication documents to allow union leaders time to digest and understand information so they are able to proactively respond to questions from their constituents

Service Clubs, Special Interest Groups, Chamber of Commerce

- Attend meetings as a guest and offer to be a guest speaker to give them the latest update on school district events, vision, goals, and progress
- Select one or two organizations you might join as an active member

Community Celebrations, Special Events, Fundraisers

- Participate and support events that align with your goals and values
- Offer to serve as a volunteer as appropriate

School Performances, Athletic Events and Exhibits, Student and Employee Awards, and Recognition Events

- Notify the planners of these events that you will attend and be prepared to make remarks if asked
- Send congratulatory notes to those recognized as appropriate

County, Regional, and Statewide Conferences and Events

- Attend professional development opportunities and invite board members and employees as appropriate
- Offer to serve on planning committees for conferences and events and make presentations on relevant topics

City Council, County School Boards, County Supervisors, National and State Legislative Representatives

- Get to know elected officials individually in their offices
- Attend and initiate meetings of elected officials to provide information and collaborate on school district and community issues

Other Community Leaders

- Get to know the police captain, fire chief, city manager, and director of parks and recreation
- Suggest regular meetings to coordinate knowledge as well as community/school events and facilities and land use
- Ensure district emergency plans are reviewed and coordinated with city events

External Communication Outlets Support

- Access local cable networks, newspapers, television, and radio outlets for proactive communication of district programs and issues
- Define clear protocols for access to these outlets in case of a high profile need to alert a wide community to emergency issues and district responses

Building Internal Leadership Capacity

School and district-level leadership positions are fundamental to a high performing school district. Savvy superintendents are always on the lookout for their next assistant principal, principal, or assistant superintendent. You can develop your own internal program to identify and prepare future administrators, and you can also seek out external potential candidates when attending conferences and meetings with other superintendents.

Key Actions

- Establish a process to identify potential leaders in the district
- Meet with aspiring leaders to determine ways to support their professional development
- Continually assess leadership assignments considering future transfer and promotion possibilities
- Encourage teachers, administrators, and board members to speak in college and university classes

Speaking From Experience

Conversations are the primary vehicle through which you carry out your daily leadership work. Sometimes at the end of a long day, it may seem that you cannot utter another word. That is a sign that you are carrying out the powerful role of a superintendent. It is also a sign that you should make some time for quiet relaxation and reflection. Share this need with your family so they can support you in your effort to rejuvenate.

Upon Reflection

My leadership actions will be . . .

Building relationships _____
_____
_____

Planning/implementing _____
_____
_____

Communicating _____
_____
_____

Monitoring/revising _____
_____
_____

Coaching/mentoring _____
_____
_____

9

Crises, the Unexpected, Caveats, and Musings

Some of our greatest strengths are our abilities to listen, tolerate ambiguity, handle conflict, and confront new challenges. Other strengths are more intangible, and have to do with core values and belief systems, with ethics and moral leadership, and with a willingness and absolute commitment to take responsibility for the next generation. We are passionate about what we do, and we love our work as advocates for children and youth.

—Johnston et al., 2002

In addition to needing a myriad of skills and knowledge, superintendents must have the good sense to know what to do and when to do it. It may not be the most elegant way to say it, but superintendents need "street smarts." Street smarts are critical all the time, but particularly during a crisis or an unexpected event. Savvy superintendents actually expect the unexpected, both positive and negative.

Stakeholders and staff member tend to see only their part of the organization. The superintendent is the one who sees the entire system and how the parts fit together, interrelate with each other, and are necessary for creating the whole.

Each morning you start your day intending to work on the district plan, a piece of the strategic plan, or another step toward advancing the mission of the district. The tasks and key actions suggested in each chapter are pieces of this plan you work on every day. Our brief explanations describing the importance are based on our knowledge of what effective superintendents do and when they are likely to do it. Key actions are not discrete tasks; rather, they are related and part of the whole and contribute to the big ideas in the district strategic plan.

Effective superintendents do tasks in the context of big ideas and concepts. They are leaders who are also skilled managers. Each task is a building block. Each leads to the next, and each is one piece that is critical to effectively executing the mission, vision, and goals of the district.

There are thousands of books on leadership. Each claims to offer exactly what you need to be a top leader. We are not claiming we have "the" answer. In fact, we think there is no "one" answer to any situation, rather, a range of options based on the circumstances. Effective superintendents decide what to do and how to do it, taking into consideration the context as well as the district's core values and principles.

Therefore, we offer our insights into five leadership traits or abilities we know are critical to the success of superintendents of public schools who create districts that focus on the success of every student. Five traits we emphasized throughout the book are: building relationships, planning/implementing, communicating, monitoring/revising, and coaching/mentoring. Developing each of these traits to a high level requires knowledge, skills, and the effective application of each of these every day. Your daily actions are important for what you accomplish and what they symbolize. As the Kouzes-Posner Second Law of Leadership says, "DWYSYWD: Do What You Say You Will Do."

A crisis puts your skills and values under the spotlight. It is an opportunity for you to learn and to teach others. And, a crisis can make or break your leadership.

We wrote this book as a group as we have our previous books. Our idea of being a leader is that we are the lead learner as well as the lead teacher and part of an integrated team. Our approach is to brainstorm, suggest, use data, reflect, and revise. Constantly listening and learning from each other is our way of being, and we recommend this approach to every superintendent.

These jobs are lonely only if we make them so. A final caveat is the importance of reaching out to others and taking care of you! Isolation is dangerous. From our own experience and from watching literally thousands of superintendents, effective ones build networks of colleagues to discuss issues, concerns, best practices, and ways to continuously improve their districts and their own performance.

The Unexpected

Effective planning means having a comprehensive, coordinated, predictable, chronological timeline. Yet, despite developing thorough, research-based, forward-looking plans, the unexpected happens. In fact, we plan for the unexpected with board-approved emergency plans. Being organized for the unexpected improves the likelihood that we will manage the unexpected effectively.

The best emergency plans include the kinds of responses and actions expected of staff, students, parents, and every government agency. Parents have to know that the school and district have a thoughtful, thorough, coordinated system with police, fire, and medical support. A complete communication plan is essential; the worst thing for parents is not knowing if their children are safe, how to pick them up if possible, or if not, who is taking care of them.

Having an emergency plan does not mean your emergency will happen the way you planned. No plan is perfect. The earthquake creates a fault that seals off part of the rescue area or evacuation route. The wildfire shifts course, and a location thought safe suddenly comes under an evacuation order. Your plan tries to account for all contingencies, but it is not possible.

In addition to a written emergency plan, you need your own personal plan of action. This requires being clear about your core values and having a match between your values and those of the board. Your steps will include who, what, when, where, and how; the sequence will depend on the nature of the crisis.

This is when your street smarts, cool head, and flexibility are critical—and tested.

Controversy surrounded the district when I arrived. I was not fully prepared for the attacks on the district from the media as well as from people inside the system. What I have come to understand is that my personal calmness and objectivity have helped me, the board, and the district to come through with most relationships intact.

—Johnston et al., 2002, p. 108

There are big emergencies, and a whole range of unexpected events, from critical and life threatening, to those that are simply annoying. The commonality? They consume time and often resources. And, they take you away from your plan.

Big Events

- Catastrophic events such as 9/11
- Downed power lines
- Fire in a school district building
- Regional fire requiring evacuation of schools, or requiring that the schools become the evacuation centers
- Student shooting—at school or in the neighborhood
- Earthquake, hurricane, tornado, flood, blizzard, ice storm, etc.

Serious Events

- Death of a student, staff member, board member
- New state law with an immediate implementation timeline
- Plumbing or water outages
- Mid-year budget shortfall
- Sudden resignation of a key staff member
- Recall campaign of a majority of the board of education

Serious Issues That Can Catch You Off Guard

- Board member collaborating with others to bring a program to the district and never tells you and pretends he didn't do it
- Board member confessing to the superintendent that he is going to be indicted for filing false reimbursement papers
- Your trusted assistant superintendent, who, although married with children, is having multiple affairs—with staff members and the head of the districtwide parent organization (also married with children)
- A student is deemed academically ineligible halfway through the sports season, causing his team to forfeit all the wins to date

- The local newspaper reporter, who fancies himself Woodward or Bernstein, barges into your office demanding to see, and perhaps print, the update you send to the board each Friday

Small Things—From Annoying to Funny

- The well-known rambler who visits every public venue to rant on his latest favorite issue
- The man who brought his wife's ashes, set them on the podium, and as he continued speaking, did not notice the urn was sliding off the podium
- A man addressing the board when his pants fell, and to make it worse, he was left standing in ruffled, pink underwear
- A board member who, during the board comment time, suggested the students' leftover food be placed around the edges of the playground so homeless persons could eat it; the board president and her fellow dumbfounded board members turned to the superintendent to respond; she did her best to dignify the suggestion while pointing out the obvious (to everyone else) difficulties of doing the well-intentioned act
- The community member who calls and wants you to stop the blimp that is flying over the city because it is advertising beer
- The water polo team that ran down the track "flashing" the superintendent (with Speedos on!) during the halftime welcoming speech of the first intra-district football game with the entire community attending

We share these examples not to be silly or frivolous, but because they really happen and you must handle them. How you do it builds your reputation as a calm, effective, smart leader, or diminishes it. Missteps handling smaller issues chip away at your reputation; missteps in big ones can be fatal to your career.

To handle crises from large to small, leaders must know themselves. Everyone looks to the leader for guidance and strength.

But Then, There Are the Wonderful Things!

- A homeless student who, against all odds, graduates from high school
- The staff member who handles endless cancer treatments with grace—and fortunately is in remission

- The board that stands firm on an issue despite great pressure to change because it is in the best interest of all students, not a few privileged ones or the loudest interest group
- The new neighbor next door who says, "I know you; you signed my high school diploma ten years ago!"
- The once low-performing school that increased its students achievement every year, becoming an award winner and the pride of the community
- The math-science and performing arts magnet schools that drew students with special interests and talents, and sparked the curiosity and achievement of others
- A graduate from sixty years ago who died without a family and whom in gratitude for the public education he received, left one million dollars to a scholarship fund for "the children of the community"

Keep track of these victories—the big ones and the little ones. Have a treasure box of photos, notes, articles clipped from the newspaper, and school bulletins. When times get difficult, close your office door, sit down, and open the box. Look through a few of these treasures, smile, and refresh yourself to continue the good work that matters so much to children's lives.

A Word About You

Our culture seems to laud those leaders who work, work, and work some more. Of course you must work hard, but if that is all you do, you have no time to reflect, revise, and think. As Ronald Heifetz writes in *Leadership Without Easy Answers*, "Working amidst the cacophony of a multiple-band dance floor, one needs a sanctuary to restore one's sense of purpose, put issues in perspective, and regain courage and heart"(1994, p. 273). We cannot think if all we are doing is racing from one event to the next meeting.

Creating a balanced life is a lifelong challenge for most of us who choose a career in school leadership, but it is a goal we must always pursue. Education is about people—all those who place their trust in you and your leadership. Your family and friends are important too! Moreover, you are important. You must take care of yourself as you do those who are precious to you.

Take time for yourself. Plan for it and calendar it, as you plan for everything else, or your personal time will disappear.

We wrote this book with the goal of helping superintendents, aspiring superintendents, school board members, and interested others be more effective in creating and leading schools where every student can learn and grow and reach his or her potential. We believe that effective planning and organizing is essential to managing well. Planning and organizing are not ends; they are tools. These tools contribute to the ability to be effective leaders, so that staff and stakeholders know they are contributing to student achievement and well-being.

We hope the ideas and suggestions presented in this book will make a positive contribution to the fulfillment of our passion and yours of improving student achievement in school districts across the nation.

Resources

Resource A. School Inspection Sheet

School Inspection Sheet			
School Site _____	Inspector _____ Date _____		
	RATINGS		
Exterior	**Good**	**Fair**	**Poor**
Fences			
Gates			
Landscape			
Playgrounds (detail)			
Asphalt			
Track and Field Areas			
Tennis Courts			
Swimming Pool			
Stairs/Decks/Landings			
Roofing			
Gutter/Roof Drains			
Relocatables (detail)			
Shade Structure (take photo)			
Update plot plan			
Interior			
Classrooms (ceilings)			
Auditorium			
Restrooms			
Library			
Gymnasium			
Locker Rooms			
Miscellaneous			
Electrical Systems			
HVAC Systems			
Structural			
Doors and Windows			
Carpet			
Paint			
Signage			
Energy Management			
Number of Appliances			
Classrooms Used for Storage			

Copyright © 2009 by Corwin Press. All rights reserved. Reprinted from *The Superintendent's Planner: A Monthly Guide and Reflective Journal* by Gloria L. Johnston, Peggy Lynch, Rene S. Townsend, Gwen E. Gross, Lorraine M. Garcy, Patricia B. Novotney, and Benita Roberts. Thousand Oaks, CA: Corwin Press, www.corwinpress.com. Reproduction authorized only for the local school site or nonprofit organization that has purchased this book.

Resource B. School Readiness Inspection Sheet

School Readiness Inspection Sheet
Summer _____

Inspected: _____

Date of Inspection: _____

Inspection Team:

District Office Staff Member: _____

Principal: _____

Maintenance Rep: _____

Operations Rep: _____

PERSONNEL ISSUES:

Teachers Hired—Adequate #:   Yes ____ No ____

Remarks _____

_____

Staff Hired—Adequate #:   Yes ____ No ____

Remarks _____

_____

Other Personnel Issues:

Remarks _____

_____

CURRICULUM AND INSTRUCTION:

Textbooks—Adequate #:   Yes ____ No ____

Remarks _____

_____

Classroom Supplies—Adequate #:   Yes ____ No ____

Remarks _____

_____

Other Curriculum and Instruction Issues:

Remarks _____

_____

SAFETY ISSUES:

Campus Supervisors Hired?   Yes ____ No ____ N/A ____

Remarks _____

_____

School Resource Officer Assigned (Secondary)? Yes ____ No ____
                                              N/A ____

Remarks _____

_____

(Continued)

(Continued)

Student ID System? (Secondary)   Yes _____ No _____

Remarks _____

_____

Other Safety Issues _____

OPERATIONS ISSUES:

Clean/Ready?   Yes _____ No _____

Remarks _____

_____

Custodial Supplies—Adequate #:   Yes _____ No _____

Remarks _____

_____

Grounds Clean/Ready?   Yes _____ No _____

Remarks _____

_____

Safety/Maintenance Repairs Done?   Yes _____ No _____

Remarks _____

_____

Other M&O Issues:

Remarks _____

_____

Overall M&O Condition of Rooms:

Main Office—Acceptable?   Yes _____ No _____

Remarks _____

_____

MPR/Gym—Acceptable?   Yes _____ No _____

Remarks _____

_____

Library—Acceptable?   Yes _____ No _____

Remarks _____

_____

Cafeteria—Acceptable?   Yes _____ No _____

Remarks _____

_____

Play Structures—Acceptable?   Yes _____ No _____

Remarks _____

_____

Restrooms—Acceptable?   Yes ____ No ____

Remarks _____

_____

Classrooms—Acceptable?   Yes ____ No ____

Remarks _____

_____

Classrooms Not Acceptable?   List Room Numbers With Remarks

_____

_____

_____

_____

_____

_____

_____

_____

Other Issues Not Covered Above

Remarks _____

_____

_____

_____

_____

_____

Copyright © 2009 by Corwin Press. All rights reserved. Reprinted from *The Superintendent's Planner: A Monthly Guide and Reflective Journal* by Gloria L. Johnston, Peggy Lynch, Rene S. Townsend, Gwen E. Gross, Lorraine M. Garcy, Patricia B. Novotney, and Benita Roberts. Thousand Oaks, CA: Corwin Press, www.corwinpress.com. Reproduction authorized only for the local school site or nonprofit organization that has purchased this book.

Resource C. Summary of School Readiness Inspections

Summary of School Readiness Inspections				
Reported by _____ Date _____				
Please note any accomplishments or concerns in each area.				
School	**Personnel Issues**	**Curriculum/ Instruction**	**Grounds/ Buildings**	**Safety/Other Observations**
Sample: Woods School	Need 1 custodian. All teachers hired.	Open Court materials have not arrived.	Playfield needs to be repaved. Classrooms are clean and ready for student occupancy.	Bushes near exit need to be cut back—potential hiding place. Master schedule has been completed.

Copyright © 2009 by Corwin Press. All rights reserved. Reprinted from *The Superintendent's Planner: A Monthly Guide and Reflective Journal* by Gloria L. Johnston, Peggy Lynch, Rene S. Townsend, Gwen E. Gross, Lorraine M. Garcy, Patricia B. Novotney, and Benita Roberts. Thousand Oaks, CA: Corwin Press, www.corwinpress.com. Reproduction authorized only for the local school site or nonprofit organization that has purchased this book.

Resource D. Key Actions Checklist

July and August Key Actions Checklist
___ Clean out your files and desk; ask your administrative assistant/secretary to do the same
___ Review last year's calendar and consider revisions and additions
___ Prepare your personal calendar/PDA for the year
___ Review your personal organization system
___ Meet with district-level administrators and review department accomplishments and preview actions plans for the new year
___ Determine dates for all internal district meetings for the year
___ Determine your agenda and discussion topics for your first meetings of the year with principals, teachers, classified staff, board members, parents, and community members
___ Publish annual mandatory legal notices
___ Review and update student and personnel board policies
___ Plan to leave town for at least part of your vacation time
___ While on leave, turn off your cell phone and computer
___ Designate a person to serve as "acting superintendent" while you are gone
___ Tell only your administrative assistant, your designee, and the board president where you can be reached
___ Develop an exercise plan for the year—and start it now
___ Calendar family vacations or special events for the year
___ Schedule your annual physical
___ Determine a process to inspect schools for readiness and prepare documentation and procedures for follow up as needed
___ Update and revise emergency contact information and procedures
___ Review/revise disaster preparedness plans and emergency services
___ Calendar a date to conduct a mock disaster exercise during the school year
___ Review safety plans for each school campus
___ Finalize plans for school registration, transportation, and food service plans
___ Finalize new student orientation plans
___ Ensure a detailed, inspiring new staff orientation is ready for presentation prior to the beginning of the school year that includes information regarding the history, culture, and organization of the district
___ Ensure new staff are well informed about the roles and responsibilities of their positions and how they are expected to contribute to the goals of the district
___ Identify and assign mentors/coaches for new staff as needed
___ Determine what district-level staff will do to support opening day and clarify responsibilities and assignments
___ Review with the school board members and school administrators protocols regarding campus visits from parents, board, and community members
___ Communicate with city officials, police, fire, etc., regarding opening day and provide them with a calendar of events for the school year

(Continued)

(Continued)

___ Review cooperative agreements with other agencies for any necessary or desired modifications

___ Finalize the list of staff to be evaluated during the year and the process to be used

___ Review board policies and administrative regulations that need to be updated and develop a calendar with timelines for revisions and additions, and for presentation for approval at board meetings

___ Pay special attention to the board policy and administrative regulations for holidays and special events

___ Write speeches and letters that convey your broad themes and goals; communicate these throughout the year

___ Finalize details of "Welcome Back" retreats or workshops for all staff, and various subgroups

___ Assess professional development needs of the leadership team

___ Determine dates for leadership team retreats or workshops for the entire year and begin to plan content based on the needs of the team

___ Plan activities for meetings and include team building activities; include others in planning and carrying out professional development

___ Develop your plan to mentor and coach new administrators

September and October Key Actions Checklist

___ Review and share student achievement results from the previous year with principals, staff members, the board, parents, and the community

___ Post student achievement data on your district Web site

___ Report on school opening to the board and the community, in writing, on your Web site and in newsletters

___ Share feedback and appreciation with those who did the hard work preparing schools for a successful opening

___ Develop key points about achievement, budget, and facilities that you want to share with every constituency

___ Convene your first meetings with staff, parents, community members, union leaders, and administrators

___ Hold your first principals' meeting to share issues, concerns, and accomplishments from the school opening

___ Reach out to the media to share the excitement of school starting and to set the tone for the year

___ Communicate clear expectations and processes for staff evaluation

___ Ensure all district and site administrators understand the evaluation procedures for teaching and support staff

___ Ensure all staff have been notified regarding evaluation timelines

___ Discuss with all administrators the process for their evaluations

___ Review any employees about whom other administrators have concerns

___ Meet with new administrators to review goals and expectations for their assignment

___ Ask board members for feedback on those you directly supervise and evaluate

___ Review prior evaluations of those who report directly to you

___ Meet with each person whom you evaluate to discuss the year's goals

___ Prepare clear and concise materials and messages about the district and distribute it to all board candidates

___ Plan and hold a workshop for all board candidates, and involve appropriate staff members

___ Work with the current board to determine how, or whether, they will participate in the workshop

___ Review election guidelines and legal information with staff

___ Educate (thoroughly and carefully) administrative staff on the politics of the election

___ Serve as a resource to staff should they have questions about the election

___ Offer to meet with candidates individually and provide identical information to each one

___ Think about how you will handle challenging election issues

___ Use discretion in dealing with the press, who may ask you about the candidates or the election, keeping in mind you work for whoever is elected

___ Plan for possible changes in board membership

___ Participate in welcome-back events

___ Schedule community presentations with consistent messages related to the new school year

___ Thank publicly and privately those who organized all opening activities

___ Develop your school site and department visitation schedule

___ Communicate your expectations for the school site and department visits (e.g., visit classes, discuss goals, review data)

___ Review back-to-school night activities, inviting board, superintendent, and district office staff participation

___ Make an initial assessment of how your leadership team is following through on the vision and direction of the district

November and December Key Actions Checklist

___ Develop a survey for new members regarding interests, goals, and focus areas for their board service so you have a written record of this data

___ Spend time with individual board members to learn their personal goals and aspirations for their board service

___ Establish agreements with board members regarding the most effective way to communicate with each of them

___ Spend ample time with each new member, providing detailed orientation materials and an opportunity for them to ask questions to help them understand all aspects of the district's operation

___ Continue to educate them throughout their board tenure

___ Schedule one-on-one board member meetings in advance of the annual organizational meeting

___ Schedule pre-conferences prior to board meetings for new and current board members to ensure that they have adequate preparation for agenda issues, particularly current challenges so they are prepared and never surprised

___ Be proactive and make contact with new board members every week

___ Develop a system to document and record interests, goals, questions, and requests for information to assure a running record of board communication

(Continued)

(Continued)

___ Write a detailed memo to yourself titled "Board Members' Interests"; update and refer to it frequently

___ Treat all board members alike and provide the same information requested by one to all

___ Introduce and put board members out front in meetings with constituents and groups

___ Facilitate collaborative relationships among all board members; acknowledge individual strengths and contributions to the board as a collective body

___ Celebrate the board and superintendent partnership with retreats and social events that focus on building relationships leading to more effective work on behalf of students

___ If your board relationship is not working effectively, take proactive steps to seek support and guidance from a trusted colleague, your professional organization, or consultants who specialize in board–superintendent relationships

___ Review the budget early in the current year and develop a communication plan to share with constituent groups

___ Engage district personnel or finance committee in proactive planning while monitoring the current year's budget status

___ Review budget guidelines and protocols to determine needs and make modifications

___ Communicate budget status with existing district and/or community budget advisory committees

___ Develop tasks for appropriate budget committees

___ Obtain financial and business operations updates and advisories from professional organizations

___ Offer your time to communicate the message to community groups

___ Develop and use a consistent, jargon-free, user-friendly, one-page budget document that provides a clear picture of the current status of the budget

___ Schedule quarterly and mid-year meetings and retreats for administration and the board to review goals and accomplishments

___ Review all student performance data to determine high priority curricular needs

___ Schedule site-by-site meetings with principals to provide an in-depth overview of student performance data and assist them in developing action plans in response to needs

___ Design a system where appropriate persons review and document accomplishments related to instructional programs

___ Develop annual school performance reports for wide distribution

___ Review the curriculum development process

___ Review and approve needed course catalog and curriculum revisions

___ Review extra- and co-curricular programs

___ Engage the board and all construction, facilities, maintenance and operations, and site-based staff members in identifying and recommending facility needs

___ Work with business and fiscal service personnel or consultants in identifying and defining all funding source options

___ Develop estimates of costs for meeting each facility's needs

___ Estimate the amount of money available from each funding source

___ Create an implementation plan that establishes a schedule to obtain funding from the selected sources and then ensure that funds are spent in time to make certain that work is completed to meet identified needs

___ Track, adjust, and communicate actions to allow for ever-changing conditions

January and February Key Actions Checklist

___ Gather information from trusted colleagues and professional organizations who can provide materials and insight regarding various approaches to the strategic planning process

___ Determine the needs of the organization by creating a planning process that matches the unique needs of your district

___ Outline the process and format, noting timelines and including individuals and groups in the goal-setting efforts, so there is a clear understanding of the various steps that will be taken to complete the plan

___ Develop an organizational chart that communicates the message about institutional priorities and relationships to interested groups

___ Print the completed strategic planning outcomes on visual documents that can be posted and shared through various communication links and venues

___ Review strategic plan progress and accomplishments on an ongoing basis and establish revised priorities and "course corrections" as needed

___ Interpret state budget projections and the impact on the district

___ Attend workshops designed to provide guidelines to districts regarding new budget initiatives

___ Finalize the district budget planning master calendar for board approval

___ Design a budget communication document that explains complex information in an easily understood format

___ Schedule board retreats and study sessions to review the budget for the coming year

___ Develop "road show" presentations throughout the community to address budget issues for appropriate constituent groups

___ Develop a master responsibility chart to outline the department leaders who have responsibility for each curriculum area

___ Develop month-by-month lists of specific tasks and focus areas that the educational services leadership team is responsible for accomplishing

___ Survey staff development needs for all school sites to determine multiyear needs for training support for employees

___ Review curriculum material and the textbook adoption cycle

___ Prioritize the curricular areas to be addressed during coming school year

___ Institute student assessment programs in all content areas to provide longitudinal data on student performance

___ Compile detailed data documents individualized by school, grade level, content area, and student in order to develop instructional support programs for each student in the system

___ Monitor school site plans and assist sites in documenting accomplishments

(Continued)

(Continued)

___ Develop action plans for summer school program implementation

___ Review responsibilities and accomplishments of established councils, committees, or advisory groups related to curriculum development and goal setting

___ Develop the structure for communication of annual student performance data

___ Expand efforts to celebrate staff achievements and professionalism

___ Develop a culture of inquiry by asking questions including: Are we achieving our goals? What do we need to improve? How can we do better? Are we reaching every student?

___ Document accomplishments on a monthly basis and add a correlated list of new areas of focus that have emerged by grade level and department, by school site, and by district department

___ Set specific dates in the calendar year to review and revise the long range plan with new areas of focus for board consideration and approval

___ Celebrate and widely share accomplishments and announce with great fanfare new initiatives focused on student support

___ Define all "publics" and constituencies that would value information about the vision, goals, accomplishments, and critical issues facing the district

___ Create a calendar of speaking engagements with the numerous groups that represent your key community leaders

___ Prepare a board briefing on the State of the District and present it at board meetings, school sites, and district departmental meetings

___ Begin planning and gathering information for an expanded version of the State of the District for the board–superintendent mid-year retreat

___ Publish the State of the District in a communitywide newsletter

___ Write an article about the district's accomplishments for email distribution, for local newspapers, school newsletters, and for the district's Web site

March and April Key Actions Checklist

___ Review three-year budget and expenditure histories for patterns

___ Review current year expenditures by program for budget and expense alignment

___ Meet with the finance committee to review their recommendations for the board

___ Formulate budget goals and assumptions for the next year.

___ Compile budget requests from department heads and principals

___ Review finance committee recommendations and district staff requests with board

___ Determine the board's priorities for meeting student needs

___ Review the tentative budget with cabinet members

___ Review additions and corrections to the new budget document with division managers

___ Review budget adoption timelines with board for the next school year

___ Meet with the business division staff to determine the status of summer facilities improvement projects

___ Review the status of five-year facilities master plan with the board

___ Place bids and quotes for capital projects on the board agenda for review and approval

___ Set priorities for facilities upgrades when funds are limited

___ Communicate priorities and timelines to staff and community

___ Determine the status of projects that face delays

___ Work with the business division to develop alternate timelines when projects are re-bid or delayed.

___ Provide a reason and new timeline for principals when projects at their schools are delayed.

___ Prepare for board action on non-reelection of certificated and classified personnel

___ Ensure that layoff notices are board approved and delivered on time and with sensitivity

___ Meet with union leaders regarding layoffs that affect members of their associations

___ Meet with human resources staff to determine the status of recruitment efforts

___ Prepare board agenda items if additional recruitment trips require approval

___ Meet with business and human resources division leaders to ensure coordination of budget detail, personnel needs, and requests

___ Develop plans for filling vacant administrative positions, promotions, or transfers

___ Meet with the leaders of the curriculum and instruction unit to plan for summer school, summer inservice, and new or revised curriculum projects

___ Place new course plans and textbook adoption recommendations on the board agenda for approval and public review

___ Review the business division's status with respect to ordering, processing, and delivering instructional materials and equipment for the new school year

___ Review the assessment/evaluation department's plans for assisting schools with the state testing programs

___ Send a letter to parents emphasizing the importance of state testing programs and solicit their cooperation and support

___ Determine important topics/issues to explore during the board workshop/retreat/advance; share suggestions with the board

___ Select the workshop/retreat planning team and provide budget parameters

___ Ensure the planning team matches the suitability of a consultant(s) based on identified needs of the group before engaging services

___ Ensure a venue is selected that will enhance outcomes and is within budget

___ Ensure that the planning team builds in an appropriate evaluation of the workshop/retreat and has a plan for rapid turnaround of results

___ Plan a social occasion to include all leadership team members, their guests, and the board. If you have space, host the event in your home

___ Establish your own professional development plan for the year

___ Schedule sufficient time to meet with each administrator you evaluate

___ Establish an annual calendar for evaluations

(Continued)

(Continued)

___ Require administrators to provide written documents regarding their contribution to the district's vision, mission, and goals; their personal goals and objectives; and, if appropriate, documents reflecting their accomplishments relative to state or other standards for administrators at least two weeks in advance of your scheduled evaluation conference

___ Prepare a draft evaluation based on your document review and personal observations

___ Review the evaluation with the administrator and seek further input

___ Modify final evaluation documents for the administrator's signature

May and June Key Actions Checklist

___ Complete and update all budget assumptions and projections

___ Share the proposed budget with the leadership team, union leaders, all staff or staff representatives, parents, and the media

___ Ensure public input is communicated to staff and the board

___ Review latest enrollment projections

___ Communicate changes to the board immediately

___ Determine interview process and timeline and identify who will participate on the interview team for various positions

___ Interview all administrative finalists; in smaller districts you may interview all teaching finalists

___ Ensure re-employment of staff, i.e., renewal of administrative contracts

___ Provide the board with copies of the evaluation instrument and timelines

___ Provide the board with data and narrative on the accomplishments—or lack of—of the year's goals prior to the meeting

___ Offer to respond to any individual board members' questions prior to the evaluation meeting

___ Include in your documentation proposed goals for the coming year for the board's consideration, as well as areas you believe you need to address re: your performance

___ Send the board a copy of the board–superintendent protocols; part of the superintendent's review should be a board self-review of its adherence to the agreed-upon operating procedures; if protocols do not exist, recommend a goal for the next year to establish these

___ Schedule enough time for a thorough, thoughtful discussion

___ Recommend having an outside consultant facilitate the review session to allow you and all board members to participate fully and to keep the session on target through completion

___ Have the facilitator perform several important tasks: assist the board in having discussions, mediating differences of opinion to bring the board to consensus on direction for the future, and do the difficult work of writing the evaluation draft for the board's review

___ Ensure the board completes the evaluation in writing and announces the result of its evaluation; in addition to meeting their contractual responsibilities, announcing the completion of the evaluation demonstrates the board's commitment to performance reviews and accountability

___ Address any potential changes to your employment contract; a facilitator can help with this since it can be difficult to negotiate one's own contract

___ Have the board extend your contract upon a satisfactory (or excellent!) review and announce it at the meeting and in a press release; this is an opportunity for the board to recognize the work you are doing and let the staff and public know they support you and the direction of the district

___ Set goals and/or focus areas for the coming year and write this into the evaluation as part of the next year's performance review

___ Have every board member sign the evaluation, or in the case of a split opinion, the board president will sign

___ Have the facilitator prepare a letter of recommendation signed by all board members based on the evaluation; the letter goes in your personnel file—you never know when it will be useful

___ Consider with the board if there is a better time of year to do your annual review; perhaps after the major student data information is available is a better time than the end of the school year

___ Spend quality time with each individual board member

___ Ask for their thoughts and insights about the goals and direction of the district

___ Consider a breakfast or lunch meeting for a more casual setting; take each member to the same location to avoid concerns of favoritism

___ Keep a record of their thoughts and ideas and how you might address them, or if you should

___ Make sure you have every important date on your calendar

___ Make sure all board members have a complete schedule of year-end events well in advance

___ If you and/or a board member is going to speak at an event, be sure you know the theme, amount of allotted time, where to sit, and any other expectations or requests

___ When there are conflicts in dates for events, develop a plan for board member attendance at each event so no school is left out

___ Do the same regarding coverage of events by you and your senior administrative leaders

___ Keep open time on your calendar for time to address a wide variety of difficult issues

___ Review policy on graduation requirements and make sure it includes a processes for who walks and doesn't walk at graduation and how you will deal with parent concerns; ensure that the policy is communicated at the beginning of the senior year

___ Review procedures on what to say to personnel who want to discuss why they are not being asked back for the following year

___ Review process that teachers can use to communicate concerns about their administrator

___ Review classroom and building cleaning and repair schedules with maintenance and operations staff

___ Monitor field renovations; ensure these have been worked through with city, parks and recreation, boys and girls clubs, and other partners' staff so everyone knows the plan for summer use

___ Review professional development activities with instructional staff; ensure activities are in line with district goals and build on prior learning

(Continued)

(Continued)

___ Put professional development activities on your calendar and plan to attend several, staying an hour or the entire time, not just dropping in

___ Have appropriate staff, including principals, review student discipline policies and prepare recommended improvements

___ Ensure business and purchasing staff order time-sensitive purchases so they arrive for school opening

___ Prepare the list of accomplishments for the current year and plan to highlight and celebrate these as you go into the new school year

___ Determine broad themes and goals you will communicate to all stakeholders throughout the coming year

___ Begin thinking and planning about the leadership team's retreat (or advance, or convocation, as some districts call them)

___ Meet with leaders of parent association groups to gather dates their major events for the coming year

___ Get input from all schools and related community organizations to build a districtwide calendar of events; include board meeting, strategic planning, and other critical committee dates

___ Communicate the district calendar broadly

___ Have back-to-school nights and other critical school events on your personal calendar

___ Make sure all board members have these events on their calendars and encourage them to attend as much as their schedules allow

___ Review the calendar regularly and publish updates

___ Use the calendar as a basis for developing the next year's calendar; it can be an effective "tickler" file

___ Review and revise communications documents such as: finger tip facts, the Web site, key communicators email list, and press releases

___ Meet with local reporter(s) to review upcoming year-end events, inviting coverage

___ Learn about new reporters and begin to get to know them

___ Ask reporters about deadlines; let them know you will make every effort to call them back to meet a deadline on an important story

___ Prepare at least a draft, if not the final, district report for the year; fall is also a good time to release the report

___ Prepare a draft of the summative evaluation using a variety of data, including the individual's self-assessment

___ Meet with each person to review and discuss the evaluation; have a very frank conversation about accomplishments and goals for the next year and beyond; this is a collaborative process, but you make the final decisions

___ Develop an improvement plan with anyone about whom you have concerns, laying out specific goals, activities, timelines, and means of assessing accomplishment

___ For those achieving at a high level, work with them to develop next steps as well as a continuous improvement plan. What are their aspirations? How can you provide them the opportunities in new areas to prepare them for their next position?

___ Brief the board on your assessment of leadership personnel privately

___ Provide a final, written evaluation to each person and give a copy to human resources for placement in their files

___ Review minutes of the year's board meetings and list routine and special topics for the coming year

___ Prepare a rough draft of a 12-month board meeting calendar of major topics by department aligned with district goals.

___ Send the draft to senior staff and principals to determine potential conflicts with religious holidays, major school events, professional development days, etc.

___ Have senior staff review the year and prepare a draft of their department's 12-month calendar for your review

___ Approve senior staff vacation so the district has leadership coverage at all times

___ Be sure the board and senior staff know when your vacation is and who will be in charge in your absence

The Routine and Expected Key Actions Checklist

School Board Meetings

___ Pre-plan using a 12-month calendar, an agreed-upon template for the agenda, and involve an agenda planning team

___ Pay attention to logistics and prepare for the unexpected

___ Carefully design the board packet for each meeting

___ Communicate the agenda widely and make sure board members are prepared for the meeting

___ Conduct each board meeting as though it is the most important one; at that point it is

___ Debrief board meetings with staff and list tasks and assignments

Principals and District Office Staff

___ Schedule regular meetings (weekly/biweekly/monthly) and plan each meeting with the outcome in mind and a carefully detailed agenda to support the outcome

___ Include participants meaningfully and use their valuable time wisely

___ Give participants opportunities to problem solve and share their expertise and suggestions regarding initiatives

___ Allow participants time to have their questions answered and respond to rumors and anxieties

Individual District and School Administrators

___ Schedule weekly or biweekly meetings to ensure you are up to date regarding school and department issues and concerns

___ Review progress toward meeting annual goals and professional development

Campus and Classroom Visits

___ Schedule regular meetings to address issues and concerns and collaborate on initiatives

___ Review data and progress toward meeting district goals

___ Follow up site visits with short emails and notes to staff and site leadership highlighting positive observations

(Continued)

(Continued)

Community Members (City Officials, Elected Officials, Business Leaders, Community Leaders, Other Education Leaders)

___ Schedule meetings as needed to address issues and concerns

___ Create ways to collaborate on communitywide initiatives

___ Share data and progress toward meeting district goals

External Experts and Consultants

___ Schedule meetings to ensure you are kept up to date on the status of deliverables and timelines regarding curriculum audits, school construction, professional development, coaching, etc.

___ Meet as needed with legal counsel to review school or department issues and new legislation, as well as discuss legal cases that have potential impact for your district

Student Achievement

___ Review district formative benchmark scores, attendance, discipline, and truancy data, grade point averages, AP and SAT scores, and any other relevant student information

___ Meet with principals to discuss progress and/or concerns and plan follow up action as needed

___ Define structure and key dates for completion of site-based school improvement action plans

Budget

___ Review monthly income and expenditures and compare to budget projections

___ Review student enrollment data

___ Review all budget targets and plan follow-up action as needed

Operations and Facilities Master Plan

___ Review operations issues, responses, and actions

___ Review facilities targets against timelines and budgets and plan follow-up action as needed

___ Update plans with established timelines to assure that issues are addressed in a timely manner

Human Resources

___ Review position controls, open positions, and hiring status

___ Review human resources issues such as grievances, suspensions, and complaints and plan follow-up action as needed

Professional Development

___ Review status of ongoing professional development and evaluations from staff

___ Review future needs, plans, and budget projections

New Initiative Stakeholder Meetings

___ Plan visits to schools; local civic, professional, and business groups; and other community-based groups to discuss new initiatives and progress in the school district

___ Convene planning or advisory groups that were involved in new initiative development and provide updates on progress

Curriculum Development, Instruction, and Assessment

___ Review curriculum work, instruction changes, and progress in meeting benchmarks

___ Conduct classroom walkthroughs with administrators (and teachers) to monitor curriculum and instruction improvements

___ Review progress in developing school-based and district assessments of student achievement

___ Attend grade-level team or department meetings to hear about teacher ideas, collaboration, and response to student learning

Communication Plan

___ Review all elements of your communication plan including contacts with board members, administrators, teachers, staff, students, and community

___ Update organizational and responsibility charts as needed

___ Schedule meetings with the media personnel

___ Continually assess all emergency planning processes and proactively review and practice all protocols and procedures

___ Review guidelines regarding use of site phones, cell phones, and out-calling phone systems for parent communications

___ Update district and site Web sites, intranet resources, and electronic communication processes within the district, outside groups, and agencies

Union Leaders

___ Meet regularly to keep lines of communication and information open and accessible with a focus on interest-based problem solving approaches

___ Share areas of concern and collaborate on strategies to resolve problems

___ Provide "heads up" copies of district communication documents to allow union leaders time to digest and understand information so they are able to proactively respond to questions from their constituents

Service Clubs, Special Interest Groups, Chamber of Commerce

___ Attend meetings as a guest and offer to be a guest speaker to give them the latest update on the school district events, vision, goals, and progress

___ Select one or two organizations you might join as an active member

Community Celebrations, Special Events, Fundraisers

___ Participate and support events that align with your goals and values

___ Offer to serve as a volunteer as appropriate

School Performances, Athletic Events and Exhibits, Student and Employee Awards and Recognition Events

___ Notify the planners of these events that you will attend and be prepared to make remarks if asked

___ Send congratulatory notes to those recognized as appropriate

County, Regional, and Statewide Conferences and Events

___ Attend professional development opportunities and invite board members and employees as appropriate

___ Offer to serve on planning committees for conferences and events and make presentations on relevant topics

(Continued)

(Continued)

City Council, County School Boards, County Supervisors, National and State Legislative Representatives

___ Get to know elected officials individually in their offices

___ Attend and initiate meetings of elected officials to provide information and collaborate on school district and community issues

Other Community Leaders

___ Get to know the police captain, fire chief, city manager, and director of parks and recreation

___ Suggest regular meetings to coordinate knowledge and community/ school events and facilities and land use

___ Ensure district emergency plans are reviewed and coordinated with city events

External Communication Outlets Support

___ Access local cable networks, newspapers, television, and radio outlets for proactive communication of district programs and issues

___ Define clear protocols for access to these outlets in case of a high-profile need to alert a wide community to emergency issues and district responses

Building Internal Leadership Capacity

___ Establish a process to identify potential leaders in the district

___ Meet with aspiring leaders to determine ways to support their professional development

___ Continually assess leadership assignments considering future transfer and promotion possibilities

___ Encourage teachers, administrators, and board members to speak in college and university classes

Copyright © 2009 by Corwin Press. All rights reserved. Reprinted from *The Superintendent's Planner: A Monthly Guide and Reflective Journal* by Gloria L. Johnston, Peggy Lynch, Rene S. Townsend, Gwen E. Gross, Lorraine M. Garcy, Patricia B. Novotney, and Benita Roberts. Thousand Oaks, CA: Corwin Press, www.corwinpress.com. Reproduction authorized only for the local school site or nonprofit organization that has purchased this book.

Resource E. Custodian Inspection Sheet

Custodian Inspection Sheet				
Items	**Above Normal**	**Normal**	**Below Normal**	**Unsatisfactory**
Office				
Desk/furniture				
Doors/walls				
Dusting				
Trash cans				
Windows				
Carpets				
Teachers' Workroom and Lounge				
Carpet				
Floor				
Sinks				
Counters				
Trash cans				
Windows				
Tables/chairs/dusting				
Nurse's Office				
Floor				
Sinks/counters				
Dusting				
Multipurpose Room				
Floor				
Carpet				
Doors/walls				
Dusting				
Windows				
Classrooms				
Doors/walls				
Chalkboards/trays				
Dusting/vents/ window ledges				
Vacuuming/corners and edges				
Carpets				
Floors				
Sinks/cabinets				
Windows				
Trash cans				

(Continued)

Custodian Inspection Sheet (Continued)				
Items	Above Normal	Normal	Below Normal	Unsatisfactory
Kitchen				
Floor/drains/dusting				
Doors/walls				
Trash can				
Custodial Rooms				
Upkeep of rooms				
Upkeep of equipment				
MSDS book				
Restrooms				
Sinks				
Mirrors				
Toilets/urinals				
Chrome fixtures				
Walls/stalls				
Vents				
Floors				
Trash cans				
Doors				
Exterior Upkeep				
Parking lot				
Sidewalks				
Blacktop				
Playground equipment				
Grass area				
Lunch area				
Drinking fountain				
Doors/walls				
Windows				
Light fixtures				
Dumpster area				
Lockers				
Library				
Carpet				
Windows				
Countertops/tables				
Dusting/trash cans				

Custodian Inspection Sheet

Items	Above Normal	Normal	Below Normal	Unsatisfactory
Woodshop				
Floors				
Windows				
Counters/sinks				
Dusting/trash cans				
Theater				
Carpet/floors				
Windows				
Trash cans/dusting				
Auto Shop				
Floors				
Countertops				
Trash cans/dusting				
P.E. Locker Area				
Floors				
Walls/shelves/vents/ mirrors				
Doors/lockers/trash cans				
Sinks/toilets/urinals/ showers/chrome fixtures				
Gymnasium				
Wood floors				
Doors/walls				
Bleachers				
Ceramics				
Floors				
Countertops/sinks				
Doors/walls				
Trash cans/dusting				
Science				
Floors				
Countertops/sinks				
Doors/walls				
Trash cans/dusting				

(Continued)

Custodian Inspection Sheet (Continued)				
Items	**Above Normal**	**Normal**	**Below Normal**	**Unsatisfactory**
Home Economics				
Floors				
Countertops/sinks				
Doors/walls				
Trash cans/dusting				
Comments:				

Inspected by: Time:

Copyright © 2009 by Corwin Press. All rights reserved. Reprinted from *The Superintendent's Planner: A Monthly Guide and Reflective Journal* by Gloria L. Johnston, Peggy Lynch, Rene S. Townsend, Gwen E. Gross, Lorraine M. Garcy, Patricia B. Novotney, and Benita Roberts. Thousand Oaks, CA: Corwin Press, www.corwinpress.com. Reproduction authorized only for the local school site or nonprofit organization that has purchased this book.

Resource F. Playground Inspection Sheet

Playground Inspection Sheet			
School Site _____ Supervisor _____	Date _____		
	Station #1	**Station #2**	**Station #3**
How many stations?			
Take Photograph			
What type of use zone material?	Sand	Sand	Sand
	Wood fiber	Wood fiber	Wood fiber
	Unitary	Unitary	Unitary
	Other	Other	Other
Condition of use zone material?	Good	Good	Good
	Fair	Fair	Fair
	Poor	Poor	Poor
Is appropriate age signage visible? example: Ages 2–5, Ages 5–12			
Overall playground condition	Good	Good	Good
	Fair	Fair	Fair
	Poor	Poor	Poor
Is playground equipment on site plan?			
Is playground ADA accessible?			
Is K area playground fenced in?			
Any apparent safety concerns?			
Sheds/Storage Containers			
How many?			
Type			
Condition	Good	Good	Good
	Fair	Fair	Fair
	Poor	Poor	Poor
Take Photograph			
Shade Structures			
How many?			
Type (cloth, wood)			
Condition	Good	Good	Good
	Fair	Fair	Fair
	Poor	Poor	Poor
Take Photograph			

Copyright © 2009 by Corwin Press. All rights reserved. Reprinted from *The Superintendent's Planner: A Monthly Guide and Reflective Journal* by Gloria L. Johnston, Peggy Lynch, Rene S. Townsend, Gwen E. Gross, Lorraine M. Garcy, Patricia B. Novotney, and Benita Roberts. Thousand Oaks, CA: Corwin Press, www.corwinpress.com. Reproduction authorized only for the local school site or nonprofit organization that has purchased this book.

Resource G. Portable or Relocatable Buildings Inspection Sheet

Portable or Relocatable Buildings Inspection Sheet			
School Site _____ Portable # _____	Date _____		
	RATINGS		
	Good	Fair	Poor
Roof			
Gutters/downspouts			
Siding type			
Skirting and vents			
Exterior paint			
Interior paint			
Carpet			
Vinyl flooring			
Ceiling			
Lighting			
Plumbing fixtures			
Restroom			
Cabinets			
Windows			
Window screens			
Doors			
Ramps			
HVAC			
Exhaust fans			

Copyright © 2009 by Corwin Press. All rights reserved. Reprinted from *The Superintendent's Planner: A Monthly Guide and Reflective Journal* by Gloria L. Johnston, Peggy Lynch, Rene S. Townsend, Gwen E. Gross, Lorraine M. Garcy, Patricia B. Novotney, and Benita Roberts. Thousand Oaks, CA: Corwin Press, www.corwinpress.com. Reproduction authorized only for the local school site or nonprofit organization that has purchased this book.

Resource H. Human Resources Annual Calendar

Human Resources Annual Calendar	
Month	**Projects/Tasks**
July	Update staffing needs based on projected enrollment
	Continue hiring of new staff
	Board agenda item to move second-year probationary teachers to tenure status
	Review last year's employee evaluations
	Develop list of employees on improvement status
	Update database of staff
	Update responsibility chart
	Update organization chart
	Prepare staff packets that include annual notifications
	Update classified hourly accounting and send to payroll
	Rerun certificated step and column movement program
August	Prepare staff evaluation lists
	Review any new education codes that effect HR
	Board agenda item on student teacher contracts with universities
	Schedule new teacher orientation
	Schedule new classified orientation
	Support administrator back-to-school retreat/advance
	Send staffing list to sites
	Send contracts to returning certificated staff
	Finish hiring of new staff
	Support district Welcome Back " activities
	Visit schools on first/second day
September	Hold required workshops on gender equity and sexual harassment
	Schedule meetings with certificated and classified union leadership
	Identify teachers for beginning teacher support and assessment program
	Send updated staffing list to sites
	Benefit meetings for staff—new and returning
	Insurance open enrollment for returning staff
	Send out reminders to staff regarding evaluation timelines
October	Review and update forms used in HR
	Prepare materials for contract negotiations with unions
	Check employee list against staffing allocations in budget
	Update employee information and send in state report
November	Review HR calendar and update
	Review and update staffing allocation formulas
	Review all employee vacation time
	Schedule employees to take vacation time based on board policy/contracts
	Review sick leave use

(Continued)

Human Resources Annual Calendar (Continued)	
Month	**Projects/Tasks**
December	Review staffing with business department
	Review list of temporary, categorical, and probationary certificated staff
	Review and update seniority lists
January	Send certificated and classified retirement guidelines to employees
	Start planning for summer school staff needs
	Review process for certificated lay off
	Plan for March 15 layoff notices
	Create hiring timeline
	Plan for career fairs
February	Have summer school applications available
	Plan for classified layoffs
	Begin posting vacancies if known
	Prepare board agenda item for layoffs
	Send leave requirements to staff
March	Send out evaluation reminders
	Hold annual staffing meetings at sites
	Establish calendars for hourly employees
	Establish calendars for 10-month and 12-month classified staff
	Send certificated retirement reminder
	Send March 15 layoff notices
April	Finalize administrator work calendar
	Review leave request and take to board for approval
	Board agenda item for temporary certificated release
	Begin hiring process for open positions
May	Classified staff 10-month notices
	Annual notification update
	Prepare HR database for next year
	Review staffing needs for next year
	Roll over staff costs for next year budget planning
	Run certificated step and column movement program
June	Review/update evaluation handbook
	Prepare retiree recognition
	Release letters to temporary staff
	Hire new staff
	Declaration of need for board agenda

*Calendar does not contain routine items that happen every month such as sending information to payroll, answering staff questions, updating staffing list, contract negotiations, advertising for substitutes, etc. Calendar should be coordinated with other district department calendars.

Copyright © 2009 by Corwin Press. All rights reserved. Reprinted from *The Superintendent's Planner: A Monthly Guide and Reflective Journal* by Gloria L. Johnston, Peggy Lynch, Rene S. Townsend, Gwen E. Gross, Lorraine M. Garcy, Patricia B. Novotney, and Benita Roberts. Thousand Oaks, CA: Corwin Press, www.corwinpress.com. Reproduction authorized only for the local school site or nonprofit organization that has purchased this book.

Resource I. Meeting Schedule

Meeting Schedule

Month	All Principals, 7:15 AM, District Ofc	Assistant Principals, 3:15 PM, Sm Brd Rm	Middle Schl Principals, 7:15 AM, Coco's	High Schl Principals, 7:15 AM, Coco's	Ldrship Team 3:15 PM, OCMS, Media Ctr	Extended Cabinet, 8:30 AM, Small Board Room	Coord Council, 3:15 PM, Large Brd Rm	Tech Cmte, 3:00 PM, D.O.	LAN Cmte, 3:15 PM, Lrg Brd Rm	Parent Rep Site Council, 12:00 PM, Small Brd Rm	BOARD MEETINGS, 6:30 PM, Large Board Room
Sept.	09/13; 09/27		9/5; 9/19	9/6; 9/20	9/10	9/25	9/26			9/24	9/6; 9/20
Oct.	10/25	10/17	10/3; 10/17	10/4; 10/18		10/23		10/10		10/22	10/4; 10/18
Nov.	11/12		11/7; 11/28	11/8; 11/29	11/5	11/27	11/28	11/14		11/26	11/8
Dec.	12/13	12/10	12/5	12/6		12/18		12/12			12/13
Jan.	01/17		1/9; 1/23	1/10; 1/24	1/14	1/23	1/16	1/9		1/28	1/17
Feb.	02/14; 02/28	02/11	2/6; 2/20	2/7; 2/21		2/26	2/20	2/13	TBD	2/25	2/7
Mar.	03/13; 03/27		3/5; 3/19	3/6; 3/20	3/10	3/25	3/19	3/12		3/24	3/6; 3/20
Apr.	04/24	04/14	4/2; 4/16	4/3; 4/17		4/29		4/16		4/28	4/17
May	05/15; 05/29		5/7; 5/21	5/8; 5/22	5/12	5/27	5/21	5/14		5/19	5/1; 5/15
June			6/4	6/05	TBD	6/24					6/5; 6/19
July					TBD						7/17
Aug.					TBD	TBD					

CABINET EVERY TUESDAY, 8:30–11:30, **EXCEPT FOR 10/15; 04/21; 06/02** (Monday instead of Tuesday)

Copyright © 2009 by Corwin Press. All rights reserved. Reprinted from *The Superintendent's Planner: A Monthly Guide and Reflective Journal* by Gloria L. Johnston, Peggy Lynch, Rene S. Townsend, Gwen E. Gross, Lorraine M. Garcy, Patricia B. Novotney, and Benita Roberts. Thousand Oaks, CA: Corwin Press, www.corwinpress.com. Reproduction authorized only for the local school site or nonprofit organization that has purchased this book.

Resource J. Certificated Administrator Evaluation Form

Certificated Administrator Evaluation Form
Name:
Assignment/School:

I. Annual Goals (October–November)

Annual goals may emerge from, but are not be limited to, the State standards for administrator effectiveness, the District's Continuous Improvement Efforts, and school or program improvement targets, including one goal based on information from site-specific data meetings. It is understood that the administration at a school site has numerous normally required duties and responsibilities that lead to the improvement of performance of each student and staff member at the school.

Goals (maximum of three)
1.
2.
3.

II. Self-Reflection (May–June)

Progress toward achieving the Annual Goals form the basis for self-reflection by the administrator. By acquiring the skills, attitudes, and behaviors outlined in the State standards of administrator effectiveness, administrators have the best opportunity to achieve the mission and vision of the district.

Accomplishments and Self-Reflection on Goals

State Standard 1: SHARED VISION OF LEARNING
A school administrator is an educational leader who promotes the success of all students by facilitating the development, articulation, implementation and stewardship of a vision of learning that is shared and supported by the school community.

State Standard 2: CULTURE FOR STUDENT LEARNING AND PROFESSIONAL GROWTH
A school administrator is an educational leader who promotes the success of all students by advocating, nurturing, and sustaining a school culture and instructional program conducive to student learning and staff professional growth

State Standard 3: ORGANIZATION AND MANAGEMENT
A school administrator is an educational leader who promotes the success of all students by ensuring management of the organization, operations, and resources for a safe, efficient, and effective learning environment.

State Standard 4: COLLABORATION WITH DIVERSE FAMILIES AND COMMUNITIES
A school administrator is an educational leader who promotes the success of all students by collaborating with families and community members, responding to diverse community interests and needs, and mobilizing community resources.

State Standard 5: PERSONAL ETHICS AND LEADERSHIP CAPACITY
A school administrator is an educational leader who promotes the success of all students by modeling a personal code of ethics and developing professional leadership capacity.

State Standard 6: POLITICAL, SOCIAL, ECONOMIC, LEGAL, AND CULTURAL UNDERSTANDING
A school administrator is an educational leader who promotes the success of all students by understanding, responding to, and influencing the larger political, social, economic, legal, and cultural context.

Comments and/or Additional Reflection (Optional)

III. Supervisor's Comments (May–June)

Comments

Areas for Growth and/or Improvement

Areas of Unsatisfactory Performance and Specific Improvement Suggestions

---

Evaluator's Signature _____ **Date** _____

Signature by the employee indicates that this evaluation has been read and discussed with the evaluator but does not necessarily indicate agreement with all factors of the evaluation.

Employee's Signature _____ **Date** _____

Distribution: *Original to Human Resources for Personnel File; copy to Employee; copy to Evaluator*   *rev. 10/29/07*

Copyright © 2009 by Corwin Press. All rights reserved. Reprinted from *The Superintendent's Planner: A Monthly Guide and Reflective Journal* by Gloria L. Johnston, Peggy Lynch, Rene S. Townsend, Gwen E. Gross, Lorraine M. Garcy, Patricia B. Novotney, and Benita Roberts. Thousand Oaks, CA: Corwin Press, www.corwinpress.com. Reproduction authorized only for the local school site or nonprofit organization that has purchased this book.

Resource K. School Administrator Evaluation Process

School Administrator Evaluation Process

I. *Background/Philosophy*

An essential component of continued professional growth and improvement is participation in a collegial evaluation process that provides the opportunity for reflection. Toward that end, the XYZUSD administrative team is engaged in an evaluation process that allows team members, as educational leaders, to set high priority goals and to be reflective about professional contributions.

Effective administrative evaluation must be specific to the professional's role and responsibilities. As a process, evaluation is an opportunity to identify priorities, highlight successes, discuss areas of concern, and examine possible obstacles. The most valuable parts of the process are the time for personal reflection and growth that emerge from professional conversations.

To accomplish this objective, three conference periods have been established. The descriptions and timelines are provided below.

II. *The Goal-Setting Conference (October–November)*

In preparation for the initial conference, principals are encouraged to reflect on the areas listed below:

A. **State Professional Standards for Educational Leaders**

B. **Mission/Purpose.** Your school's/department's vision for the future.

C. **Priorities and Goals.** Three priorities for your school that will have the greatest impact on improving learning for all students and or the school learning community.

D. **Support.** Support needed from the superintendent, human resources, business office, or education services to achieve your school's goals.

III. *Mid-Year Walk/Talk (January–February)*

The principal/program administrator will serve as "guide" for the mid-year walk/talk. Time should be structured to include evidence of progress on goals.

- Talk about what excites you, what concerns you, successes to date, needs
- Assessment of progress toward goals
- Insights, ideas, suggestions

- Reflection on "lessons learned of late"
- Next steps

IV. *End-of-the-Year Conference and Written Summary (May–June)*
The end-of-the-year conference will serve as an end-of-the-year wrap-up. Please write a summary of your accomplishments, which should include:

- Accomplishments/successes

- Lessons learned

- Next steps

The summary with any evaluation comments and signed by the administrator and evaluator serve as the evaluation document of the year.

V. *Conclusion*
The administrator evaluation is intended to be a positive process that will provide XYZUSD administrators the opportunity to reflect on their work and its important relationship to the teaching and learning environment and student success.

Copyright © 2009 by Corwin Press. All rights reserved. Reprinted from *The Superintendent's Planner: A Monthly Guide and Reflective Journal* by Gloria L. Johnston, Peggy Lynch, Rene S. Townsend, Gwen E. Gross, Lorraine M. Garcy, Patricia B. Novotney, and Benita Roberts. Thousand Oaks, CA: Corwin Press, www.corwinpress.com. Reproduction authorized only for the local school site or nonprofit organization that has purchased this book.

Resource L. Budget Guidelines for Board and Staff

Budget Guidelines for Board and Staff

1. Specific timelines will be established for board action.

2. The district will continue to provide an effective educational program that meets federal, state, and district mandates at all grades.

3. Enhancements will be based on the greatest impact on teaching and learning.

4. Augmentation input will be gathered from parents, faculty, staff, and board.

5. Collective bargaining commitments will be honored.

6. Salary and benefit levels will continue to attract and retain qualified people.

7. Equipment replacement will be funded in relation to available resources.

8. Increases/decreases in costs of services will be provided for (i.e., gasoline, electricity, insurance, trash, debt repayment).

9. Categorical programs shall be self-supporting and, where allowable, include allocations for indirect costs. Special education is recognized as not self-supporting, but efforts will be made to this end.

10. A new goal, project, or program will specify required resources.

11. Department budgets will provide prior year actual expenditures and past years' expenditures along with the proposed budget.

12. Projections will include associated salary and fringe benefit costs within each program area, recognizing required step, column, and longevity increases for all staff.

13. All funds maintained by the district in addition to the general fund shall be included in the budget document.

14. New one-time income shall be identified and appropriated only to support expenditures that are not ongoing costs.

15. Budgeted expenditures shall not exceed income.

16. Capital improvements and preventative maintenance shall be planned to preserve the use and value of existing facilities and equipment.

17. Potential expenditures will be identified as funds become available.

18. Education Foundation, PTA, and other contributors will be encouraged to make three-year commitments.

Copyright © 2009 by Corwin Press. All rights reserved. Reprinted from *The Superintendent's Planner: A Monthly Guide and Reflective Journal* by Gloria L. Johnston, Peggy Lynch, Rene S. Townsend, Gwen E. Gross, Lorraine M. Garcy, Patricia B. Novotney, and Benita Roberts. Thousand Oaks, CA: Corwin Press, www.corwinpress.com. Reproduction authorized only for the local school site or nonprofit organization that has purchased this book.

Resource M. Budget Planning Calendar Dates

Budget Planning Calendar Dates Calendar Year _ _ _ _		
Meeting Date	**Meetings**	**Meeting Purpose**
July	Board Meeting	Approve tax lien resolutions
August	Board Meeting	Spending limit resolution
September	Finance Committee Board Meeting	Budget revisions/review of unaudited actuals
October	Finance Committee	
November	Board Meeting	Approve next year's budget guidelines
December	Board Meeting Finance Committee	Annual audit report review 1st interim report review
January	Board Meeting Meetings With Principals	Budget calendar for next year Review proposed state funding for schools Classified and certificated staffing
February	Principals' Meeting Leadership Team Board Budget Study Session Finance Committee Curriculum Meeting Asst. Principals/Counselors	Budget update, staff reductions, budget reductions
March	Certificated Notifications PTA Council Board Facilities Study Session Board Meeting Board Budget Study Session	Release of temp teachers Non-reelection of probationary employees Reassignment of administrators Layoff of certificated staff Budget update Facilities update 2nd interim report approval Review budget cut/addition recommendations
April	Certificated Staff Meeting	Certificated retirement notification
May	Board Meeting Finance Committee	Classified layoff Review of state funding for schools Review of state funding for schools
June	Board Meeting Finance Committee Board Meeting	Approve authorized signatures Review next year's DRAFT budget Review next year's DRAFT budget Approve next year's budget adoption

Copyright © 2009 by Corwin Press. All rights reserved. Reprinted from *The Superintendent's Planner: A Monthly Guide and Reflective Journal* by Gloria L. Johnston, Peggy Lynch, Rene S. Townsend, Gwen E. Gross, Lorraine M. Garcy, Patricia B. Novotney, and Benita Roberts. Thousand Oaks, CA: Corwin Press, www.corwinpress.com. Reproduction authorized only for the local school site or nonprofit organization that has purchased this book.

Resource N. Planned Priorities

Office of the Superintendent
Planned Priorities
Week of _____

- Cabinet/Agenda Setting
- All Administrators' Meeting
- Girls Math and Science Conference
- Board of Education
- Listening Visits
- Community/Public Relations

Date	Time	Subject	Place
Monday	9:00 a.m.	Cabinet	Room 228
	12:00 noon	Agenda Setting	Room 228
	1:00 p.m.	Teaching and Learning	Room 228
	3:00 p.m.	All Administrators' Meeting	Multipurpose Room
	5:30 p.m.	Meeting With Three Staff Members	Superintendent's Home
Tuesday	7:30 a.m.	Leadership and Learning	Conference Room
	9:30 a.m.	Principals	Superintendent's Office
	11:30 a.m.	Parents	Elementary School
	2:00 p.m.	Listening Visit	Superintendent's Office
	3:00 p.m.	Parents	Superintendent's Office
	4:00 p.m.	Phone Call	High School
	5:00 p.m.	Student Board Representatives High School Principals	Superintendent's Office
Wednesday	9:00 a.m.	Girls Math and Science Conference	University
	11:45 a.m.	WASC Visitation Committee Meeting	High School
	1:00 p.m.	Board Member	Superintendent's Office
	2:00 p.m.	Board Member	Superintendent's Office
	3:30 p.m.	Classroom Conversations Taping	Elementary School
	5:45 p.m.	Board of Education—Closed Session	Middle School
	6:30 p.m.	Board of Education—Public Session	Middle School
Thursday	9:00 a.m.	Campus Tour	Leadership Public School
	10:50 a.m.	Listening Visit	Middle School
	1:30 p.m.	Parent	Superintendent's Office
	3:00 p.m.	Ad Hoc Committee (Site Acquisition)	Cabinet Room
	5:30 p.m.	Union President Meeting	Chamber Office
Friday	9:00 a.m.	Meet for Chartered Bus	Facilities Operations
	10:30 a.m.	Campus Tour—High School	Out of Town
	12:00 noon	Rotary	In Town

Copyright © 2009 by Corwin Press. All rights reserved. Reprinted from *The Superintendent's Planner: A Monthly Guide and Reflective Journal* by Gloria L. Johnston, Peggy Lynch, Rene S. Townsend, Gwen E. Gross, Lorraine M. Garcy, Patricia B. Novotney, and Benita Roberts. Thousand Oaks, CA: Corwin Press, www.corwinpress.com. Reproduction authorized only for the local school site or nonprofit organization that has purchased this book.

Resource O. Sample Organization Chart

Sample Organization Chart

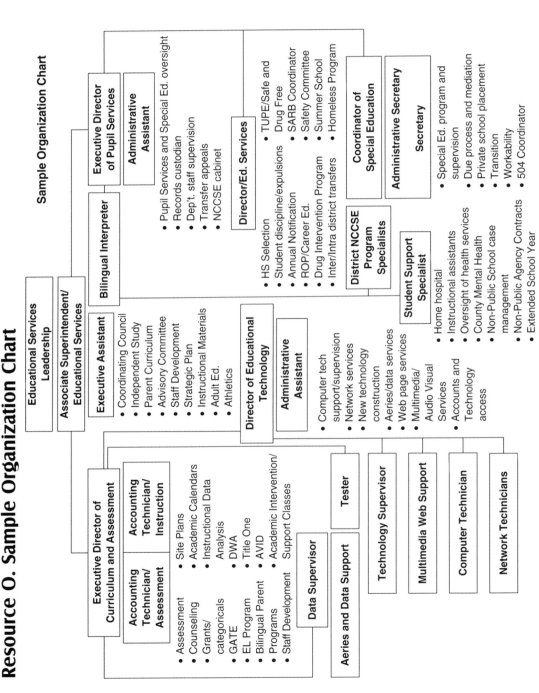

Copyright © 2009 by Corwin Press. All rights reserved. Reprinted from *The Superintendent's Planner: A Monthly Guide and Reflective Journal* by Gloria L. Johnston, Peggy Lynch, Rene S. Townsend, Gwen E. Gross, Lorraine M. Garcy, Patricia B. Novotney, and Benita Roberts. Thousand Oaks, CA:

Resource P. Information for Board Members

Information for Board Members

School District: _____
Address: _____
Main District Phone Number: _____
Superintendent: _____ Direct Phone Number: _____
Cell Phone Number: _____

E-mail Address: _____
Superintendent's Administrative Assistant: _____
Direct Phone Number: _____
E-mail Address: _____

Board Members:

Name	Office	Home Phone	Work/Cell Phone	E-mail Address
	President			
	Vice President			

Communities Served By the District:
_____

Number of Employees in the District:
Certificated: _____ Classified: _____ Confidential: _____ Management: _____

What Unions Are in Place?
Classified: _____ Certificated: _____ Administrator: _____

Grade Levels Served by the District:
Preschool _____ K–6 _____ K–8 _____ K–12 _____ 7–12 _____ 9–12 _____

Number of Students Enrolled:
Total enrollment: _____ Elementary School: _____ Middle/Jr. High School: _____
High School: _____ Continuation High School: _____ Community Day School: _____
Preschool: _____ Adult School: _____ Charter: _____ Independent Study: _____
Other enrollment: _____

Student Population:
Ethnic groups by percentage: _____ Percent of English Language Learners: _____
Percent of special education students: _____
Primary languages spoken in the home: _____
Percent of students receiving free or reduced lunch: _____

Number of Square Miles the District Covers: _____

(Continued)

(Continued)

Home to School Transportation:
Number of buses: _____ Number of miles driven each day: _____

Lunch Program:
Number of students served: _____ Number of students on free/reduced: _____

Number of Schools: Total: _____
Preschool: _____ Elementary School: _____ Middle/Jr. High School: _____
High School: _____ Continuation High School: _____ Community Day School: _____
Adult School: _____ Charter: _____ Independent Study: _____

District Office/Departments:

Department	Title/Name of Department Head	Phone Number

Standing Advisory Committees:

Committee Name	Staff Member Responsible	Board Representation
Facility Committee		
Visual and Performing Arts Committee		
Bond Oversight Committee		

District Documents:

Strategic/Long-Range Plan   General Fund Budget
Certificated and Classified Staff Handbooks Board Policies/Bylaws
District School Year Calendar   Collective Bargaining Agreements
Long-Range Facilities Plan

Current District Issues:

Issue	Status of the Issue

District Schools:

Name of School	Grades	Enrollment	Principal	Phone Number

ABOUT GOVERNANCE TEAM OPERATIONS

Board Meeting Dates, Location, and Times:

Board Officers:

Office Held	Name	Role
President		
Vice President		
Clerk		
Secretary		

Order of Items on the Board Meeting Agenda:

1. Roll Call
2. Recognition of Guests
3. Public Input
4. Correspondence
5. Consent
6. Old Business
7. New Business
8. Reports
9. Closed Session

Purpose of Public Input Section of the Board Meeting:
To allow the public to comment on topics of interest to them that they feel the Board should be aware of and possibly address at a future meeting.

Purpose of the Board Report Section of the Board Meeting:
To allow each Board member to report on activities or raise issues that they would like to see addressed at future Board meetings.

Governance Norms—How We Behave
Toward Members of the Governance Team and Others:
Embrace the "can do" attitude by looking forward (not backwards)
No surprises, give a heads up ASAP by communicating horizontally and vertically
Tough on issues, soft on people (focus on the problem, not the person)
Model desired behavior; teamwork; higher expectations; excellence; quality
Maintain confidentiality
Learning—focus discussions on student and adult learning

Governance Protocols—How We Do Business:
How the Board meeting agenda is developed and reviewed and by whom:

(Continued)

(Continued)

How the Board meeting agenda is developed and reviewed and by whom:	Sites, departments, and the Board President submit items to the Superintendent to include on the Board agenda. The Superintendent and Board President discuss and agree on items and timing.
Placing items on the Board meeting agenda:	Agenda items need to be submitted no less than eight working days prior to the Board meeting date.
Obtaining additional information about Board meeting agenda items before the Board meeting:	Call the Superintendent as soon as possible so he/she can research the issue and get the desired information. The appropriate District personnel will be directed to you.
Alerting the Board President of the desire to speak on a particular agenda item:	Call the Board President when you receive the agenda and have reviewed it.
Introducing new ideas for the Board's consideration:	Contact the Board President and Superintendent to request the item be placed on a future agenda.
Responding to staff or community complaints or concerns at Board meetings:	Acknowledge the complaint/concern. The Board President recommends the Superintendent investigate, meet with the complainant, and make the appropriate recommendation and/or take the appropriate action.
Communications between and among the Board, Board members, and the Superintendent:	The Board cannot be polled on issues outside of Board meetings. At Board meetings members should express their opinions on issues to other Board members and the public. Be aware of the Public Information Act when using e-mail and use only District e-mail. You may contact the Board President and Superintendent, beyond that may open the possibility of a closed meeting violation.
Communications between the Board and other staff:	Contact the Superintendent for information and to share concerns. The Superintendent will follow up with staff as appropriate.
Responding to community or staff complaints or concerns outside of Board meetings:	Acknowledge the complaint or concern. Ask if they have spoken with the site/department supervisor. Ask that they follow the chain of command all the way through and then call you back if not satisfied. Notify the Superintendent of the conversation.
How, when, and whom to notify about visiting school sites or participating in District activities:	Call the Superintendent who will notify the sites. While you are a VIP visitor, you are a member of the public acting alone when you visit, and all District policies and procedures apply to your visit.

Individual Board member requests for information from staff:	Contact the Superintendent for all information requests. The Superintendent will either get the information to you or direct the appropriate person to contact you. As a parent of a student, you may contact school personnel for information any other parent might request or receive.
Board member participation on District committees and in District activities:	Appointment to Board committees is made by the Board. Board members may attend committee meetings. You are a member of the public unless appointed by the Board.
When and how the Board conducts a self-evaluation:	Annual evaluation completed at the goal setting workshop following the Superintendent's evaluation.
When and how the Board evaluates the Superintendent:	As per the Superintendent's contract, on or before December 31, the Board may evaluate the Superintendent. The Superintendent will submit a recommended format.

Governance Documents:

District Policies/Bylaws	Vision, Mission, Core Beliefs	Open Meeting Laws
District Setting Direction Documents	District Budget Development Calendar	Annual Board Meeting Calendar
Governance Handbook	State Professional Governance Standards	

Board Member Benefits:

Stipend	
Health benefits	
Attending conferences/educational meetings/community events	
Reservations for conferences/workshops/District travel	
Travel expenses and reimbursements	

Copyright © 2009 by Corwin Press. All rights reserved. Reprinted from *The Superintendent's Planner: A Monthly Guide and Reflective Journal* by Gloria L. Johnston, Peggy Lynch, Rene S. Townsend, Gwen E. Gross, Lorraine M. Garcy, Patricia B. Novotney, and Benita Roberts. Thousand Oaks, CA: Corwin Press, www.corwinpress.com. Reproduction authorized only for the local school site or nonprofit organization that has purchased this book.

Resource Q. Responsibility Chart

Responsibility Chart		
Assignment	**Contact Person**	**Phone Number / E-mail**
Absence Forms, Staff		
Absence Forms, Students		
Accounts Payable		
Accounts Receivable		
Adult Education		
After-School Programs		
Agency Liaison for Student Support		
Assessment and Testing— Elementary		
Assessment and Testing— Middle		
Assessment and Testing— High School		
Beginning Teacher Support and Assessment		
Benefits		
Block Grants		
Board Meetings and Agendas		
Board Policies		
Budget Development		
Business Partnerships		
Categorical Programs		
Certificated Personnel		
Charter Schools		
Child Welfare and Attendance		
Classified Personnel		
COBRA—Consolidated Omnibus Budget Reconciliation Act		
Contracts—Business		
Contracts—Construction		
Contracts—Consultants		
Contracts—Employees		
Contracts—Nonpublic Schools		
Coordinated Compliance Review		
Counseling		

Responsibility Chart		
Assignment	Contact Person	Phone Number / E-mail
Credentialing—Teachers/ Substitutes		
Crossing Guards		
Cumulative Student Records		
Custodial Services		
Data Disaggregating		
Education Foundation		
Emergency Preparedness		
Enrollment Projections		
Evaluation of Personnel		
Expulsions		
Facilities—Construction, new and modernization		
Facilities—Use		
Food Services		
Free and Reduced Lunches		
Gifted Students		
Gifts/Donations		
Grade-Level Meetings		
Graduation Requirements		
Grant Writing		
Heath Services/Screenings		
Home Hospital Support		
Independent Study		
Injury and Illness Prevention Program		
Instructional Time/Minutes		
Kindergarten Registration		
Kindergarten Screening		
Leaves of Absence		
Liability Insurance		
Library Services		
Mail Delivery—External		
Mail Delivery—Intra District/ Schools		
Maintenance and Operations		
Music Program Support		
Office of Civil Rights Reporting		

(Continued)

Responsibility Chart (Continued)		
Assignment	**Contact Person**	**Phone Number / E-mail**
Payroll		
Personnel Directory		
Personnel—Hiring Process		
Preschool Programs		
Press Releases		
Public Records Act—Timelines		
Psychological Services		
Purchase Orders/Requisitions		
Recognition of Employees/Service Awards		
Reimbursement Procedures		
Report Cards		
Residency Verification		
Resignations		
Risk Management		
Sabbaticals		
Safety Committee—Districtwide		
School Attendance and Review Board		
School Plans		
School Resource Officers		
Section 504—Employees		
Section 504—Students		
Substitute Classified Employees		
Substitute Teachers		
Substitute Calling		
Summer School		
Suspensions		
Teacher Selections and Orientation		
Technology—Administration		
Technology—Instructional		
Technology—Database		
Technology—Budget		
Telephone System/Cell Phones		

Responsibility Chart		
Assignment	**Contact Person**	**Phone Number / E-mail**
Textbook Ordering, Inventory, and Delivery		
Transportation—Home to School		
Transportation—Special Education		
Truancy		
Uniform Complaint Procedures		
Volunteers—Processing		
Warehouse		
Web Site		
Worker's Compensation		

Copyright © 2009 by Corwin Press. All rights reserved. Reprinted from *The Superintendent's Planner: A Monthly Guide and Reflective Journal* by Gloria L. Johnston, Peggy Lynch, Rene S. Townsend, Gwen E. Gross, Lorraine M. Garcy, Patricia B. Novotney, and Benita Roberts. Thousand Oaks, CA: Corwin Press, www.corwinpress.com. Reproduction authorized only for the local school site or nonprofit organization that has purchased this book.

References

Harvey, E., Cottrell, D., & Lucia, A. (2003). *The leadership secrets of Santa Claus.* Dallas: The Walk the Talk Company.

Heifetz, R.A., (1994). *Leadership without easy answers.* Cambridge, MA: The Belknap Press of Harvard University Press.

Johnston, G. L., Gross, G. E., Townsend, R. S., Lynch, P., Novotney, P. B., Roberts, B., et al. (2002). *Eight at the top: A view inside public education.* Lanham, MD: Rowman & Littlefield.

Kouzes, J. M., & Posner, B. Z. (2007). *The leadership challenge.* San Francisco: Jossey-Bass.

O'Neill, P. T. (1991). *The Masai greeting speech.* Framingham, MA: First Parish Unitarian Universalist Church.

Townsend, R. S., Johnston, G. L., Gross, G. E., Lynch, P., Garcy, L. M., Roberts, B. B., et al. (2006). *Effective superintendent–school board practices: Strategies for developing and maintaining good relationships with your board.* Thousand Oaks, CA: Corwin Press.

Index

CORWIN PRESS

The Corwin Press logo—a raven striding across an open book—represents the union of courage and learning. Corwin Press is committed to improving education for all learners by publishing books and other professional development resources for those serving the field of PreK–12 education. By providing practical, hands-on materials, Corwin Press continues to carry out the promise of its motto: **"Helping Educators Do Their Work Better."**